Geographical Issues on Maritime Names

Special Reference to the East Sea

Geographical Issues on Maritime Names
Special Reference to the East Sea

Published in 2010
Reprinted in 2017

81, Tongil-ro, Seodaemun-gu, Seoul, 03739, Republic of Korea
book@nahf.or.kr

ISBN 978-89-6187-201-0-93900

Geographical Issues on Maritime Names

Special Reference to the East Sea

NORTHEAST ASIAN
HISTORY FOUNDATION

Publisher's Foreword

East Asian countries often find themselves at odds with one another when it comes to historical issues, even though they have a long history of shared culture, philosophical ideas and writing systems. The good neighbor policy they have pursued, in recent history, through diverse exchanges at various levels has often been tarnished by their cultural and historical pride and political interests. The ongoing territorial and historical tensions and conflicts in East Asia attest to this.

Launched in September 2006, the Northeast Asian History Foundation is committed to the extensive and in-depth study of the history of East Asian nations and peoples for the promotion of friendship and cultural and historical understanding. The goal of the foundation is to contribute to the establishment of an East Asian community characterized by a trust and cooperation that transcends antagonism and conflict.

The Northeast Asian History Foundation aims to serve as a reliable think tank with regards to the historical and territorial issues that beset East Asia and the subsequent development of appropriate long-term policies. To that end, it has strived to expand the realms of its research so as to develop and share objective historical aware-ness through the exploration and dissemination of new research topics and the sharing of the relevant findings.

Compiled by the Northeast Asian History Foundation, *Geographical Issues on Maritime Names: Special Reference to the East Sea* is the first English language publication of its kind to be released to domestic and international audiences. It is a manifestation of the foundation's concerted effort to address the issues surrounding the geographical name of the East Sea and provide a source for objective research.

What is especially noteworthy is that 17 global experts on, geographical names contributed to the publication, including former chairmen and vice chairman of the UN Group of Experts on Geographical Names (UNGEGN), chiefs of UNGEGN working groups, the former secretary-general of the Permanent Committee on Geographical Names in the United Kingdom, and scholars in related areas (geography, history, international law).

The Northeast Asian History Foundation will continue to the utmost of its capabilities, its endeavors to respond to territorial and historical issues so as to create a peaceful atmosphere for mutual prosperity.

I hope that the Northeast Asian History Foundation will serve as the driving force in strengthening academic research. I also hope that this publication in English will go some way to addressing the global awareness toward and legitimacy of the English name 'East Sea'.

Kim Dohyung, President
Northeast Asian History Foundation

Contents

A Historical Focus

International Framework

Possible Solutions

Interviews

Appendix

◆ Resolutions of the International Hydrographic
Organization

Introduction

It was in 1992 at the Sixth United Nations Conference on the Standardization of Geographical Names, held in New York, that the Korean Government for the first time officially raised in the international forum the naming issue of the sea between the Korean Peninsula and the Japanese Archipelago. Korean delegates, both governmental and academic, have since been making continuous efforts to disseminate the name "East Sea" throughout the world.

The past eighteen years of promoting the name 'East Sea' has witnessed considerable progress. Most importantly, international organizations in charge of place names or sea names, such as the United Nations Group of Experts on Geographical Names (UNGEGN) and the International Hydrographic Organization (IHO), now perceive the seriousness of this naming issue and are seeking change. Major mapmakers with international influence have also changed their policies from solely using the name 'Sea of Japan' to concurrently using the name 'East Sea' with it.

Providing convincing evidence and logic has been more effective in persuading international society rather than relying on emotional appeal. In support of the name 'East Sea', therefore, Koreans have purveyed historical and geographical justifications, toponymic principles and policies, and ramifications from similar cases, so as to place the issue in the academic arena and successfully draw the attention of experts in the field of geographical naming.

The International Seminar on Sea Names, organized by the Society for the East Sea, together with the Northeast Asian History Foundation since its establishment, has contributed to academic discussions on this sea-naming issue. Sixteen years ago, the seminar initially set out to search for a resolution to the chronic disputes between Korea and Japan on the name of the sea between them. Its scope has since evolved into a general forum for discussing principles and practices of naming seas and issues they entail in term of international standardization and documentation. The seminar's proceedings are regularly reported to the UNGEGN.

The seventeen papers in this book were carefully selected among the papers presented through the past sixteen seminars held annually since 1995. They are classified into five parts. The first part deals with general issues of naming seas. Included are issues such as defining location for maritime features (Kadmon), using an "exonym" to name a maritime object beyond a single sovereignty (Jordan), conflicts and possible solutions to issues involving maritime names used in more than two languages (Kadmon), and problems with using country names for international bodies of water (Murphy).

The second part moves on to the status quo of the names East Sea and Sea of Japan. Topics in this part look at the essence of the problem (Li), the meaning of name changes with respect to semantics (Dormels), usage of the name East Sea in scientific literature (Cherkis), and the toponymic status of the names East Sea and Sea of Japan (Kadmon).

The third and fourth parts focus on considering the naming issue in terms of history and international frameworks. The history of the name East Sea is traced in Korean history (Lee), Chinese literature (Han) and Russian research (Ganzey). International frameworks such as United Nations resolutions (Raper), policies of the UNGEGN (Atoui) and the IHO (Park) are also examined in search of implications that may offer solutions.

The last part is dedicated to possible solutions to the naming issue. Suggestions made include both "Donghae" (East Sea) and "Nihonkai" (Sea of Japan) being accepted as endonyms for the whole feature of the sea (Woodman); possibly giving separate names to separate parts to accommodate each party's perception (Choo); and using the names East Sea and Sea of

Japan concurrently like some old maps, a practice that mapmakers have recently been adopting (Shin).

This book has been edited to offer an overview of the naming issue of the East Sea so that it may serve as a textbook on the issue. Publishing such a textbook in English has been a long-held aspiration for advocates of the name East Sea. Hopefully, this publication can be developed into a series of books and thus contribute to a better understanding of toponymy for international society.

Issues of Naming Seas

The Definition of Location of Maritime Objects and Their Names

Naftali Kadmon

Is "Exonym" an Appropriate Term for Names of Features Beyond Any Sovereignty?

Peter Jordan

Bilingual and Multilingual Marine and Lacustrine Names: Consent and Dissent

Naftali Kadmon

Use of National Names for International Bodies of Water

Alexander B. Murphy

The Definition of Location of Maritime Objects and Their Names[1]

Naftali Kadmon

This paper deals with the question of defining the location of geographical items, among them maritime features, by various means and measures. Also, referring among others to the East Sea, it will show some difficulties met in the process of defining location.

An anthroponym, that is, a name of a person, relates to a 'moveable' object; its bearer can change his or her location at any moment. By way of contrast, a toponym refers in general to a fixed, immoveable, object. In order to be assigned its place in space, for example, in mapping or in a GIS (geographic information system) it must be given a spatial address.

---

1) This paper has been presented at *The 14th International Seminar on Sea Names - Geography, Sea Names, and Undersea Feature Names* (2008).

I. The Three Scales of Measurement: Nominal, Ordinal, and Quantitative

When man first began not only to relate to particular geographical objects in his environment but to convey their location to others of his species, he must have used verbal descriptions of the properties of any object in question, as well as physically pointing out its direction in relation to the speaker. An indication of distance must have come at a later stage, probably at first in terms of time and later in terms of metric distance. However, before an object can be named it must be identified. In the case of living things, which as mentioned above are mobile rather than fixed to a particular location, this usually involves describing the properties of the subject. Identifying immovable objects, and especially different objects belonging to a single category of items, must involve a definition of location – otherwise there would be no possibility of distinguishing between them. This is particularly true of topographic features which make up categories or feature classes: mountains, rivers, lakes, seas, islands, populated places and many others. Below we shall briefly investigate how the location of geographical items – which are the objects of toponymy – can be defined.

All measuring activities, in the widest sense, can be conducted on three main 'scales'. The first is the nominal scale: here, each item is distinguished from all others in the set by its nature, and therefore it can be named (hence the term *nominal*, from Latin *nomen*, name) – but not graded. Examples are soil types, human occupations or professions (disregarding income or social status!)

or countries. The second is the ordinal scale (from Latin *ordo*, order), in which items of a set can be arranged or graded in a clearly-defined progression or order, for example, by size, intensity, value etc. – but not measured quantitatively. Military ranks, university degrees or the contestants in a beauty contest are examples of items arranged on an ordinal scale, as are roads graded by arteriality or rivers by their stream order.

Finally there is the quantitative scale, on which objects can be measured in a 'metric' way, that is, with a measuring tape, thermometer, weighing scales, monetary system or other measuring device; examples are income, intelligence quotient (I.Q.), distance, angle, etc. Strictly speaking, quantitative scales can be divided into two types. Interval scales have fixed units but no intrinsically fixed origin; angles, which can be measured from any direction, are an example, as is temperature which, at least in the Centigrade and Fahrenheit scales, has different zero points. On the other hand ratio scales are those which have a 'naturally' fixed zero or point of origin, three examples being length, weight and azimuth (angle of direction, always measured clockwise from North).

In this text we shall refer to both interval scales and ratio scales under the combined heading of quantitative scales.

II. Defining Location on Different Measuring Scales

Coming now 'down to earth' and to our reference body: a place on Earth – or, for that matter, on a celestial body such as the moon or a planet–can be defined in a number of ways. Coordinates such as geographical latitude and longitude, or plane topographic coordinates such as the UTM grid (see below), constitute a quantitative definition. A named or numbered grid square such as B-5 in a town plan forms an ordinal definition, because only an orderly progression of finite-size map squares is provided as reference frame for the geographical objects, not exact measurements of arbitrary precision. Last – but earliest in historical development – is the verbal description of location, that is, by a name. Each method has its advantages and disadvantages. As shall be demonstrated, coordinates are precise to a point (and define an error square, the size of which depends on the smallest unit used in the coordinates); an ordinal grid rectangle is more comprehensive and is better understood by many readers, but includes on the average many dozens or even hundreds of names. Finally, names are still the world's primary reference system: according to Orth, approximately one billion names are being used by roughly six billion people populating the Earth.[2]

Ⅲ. Names as Locators

What, then, are the advantages of designating a geographical feature by its name? Primarily, a name is more easily remembered

2) Donald J. Orth (1987), *Organization and Function of a National Geographical Names Standardization Programme*, New York : United Nations.

by most people than a set of numbers. Secondly, in many cases some mental connotation can be attributed to the name. Thirdly, a name can indicate not only a small object such as a spring or a cave, but also a larger area such as a city or even an entire continent or an ocean. Fourthly and chiefly, a name can often supply an appreciable amount of information about the location referred to, such as the type of place it is, and in many cases about its cultural, political and historical background. And therein lay the roots of a problem of mainly cultural-historical or, in many cases political, character. Whereas coordinates in a given framework are unambiguous, names are not: a given well-defined location may be addressed by various names by different cultures or political systems, sometimes leading to friction and rivalry. Cases are, of course, too numerous to list, and a few examples may serve the purpose: the German names of towns and villages in German *Lebensraum* in French, Polish or Czech soil between the two world wars; Greek and Turkish names in Cyprus after 1974, maritime names such as the *Persian Gulf* vs. the *Arabian Gulf*; *Nihon Kai* (Sea of Japan) as against *Donghae* (East Sea), *Yam Kinneret* (Hebrew) vs. *Buḥayrat Tabarīya* (Arabic) for the Sea of Galilee in Israel. Here we encounter the first difficulty in assigning a name to a topographic item: which name or names, perhaps from among a selection of allonyms (alternative names), should be given to it?

Are there any drawbacks to designating a place only with the aid of its name, besides the lack of 'geometric' precision? Yes, there are three. Firstly, one name often refers to several geographical features. Let us take the name Bethlehem. In the Holy Land alone (Israel/Palestine) there are two Bethlehems: one South of Jerusalem, also called Bethlehem-Judah in the Bible (Judges 19 : 2), and one in Galilee (Joshua 19 : 15). But we find cities and towns carrying the name Bethlehem (or its derivatives, that is, its conversions and exonyms) in many other countries. In the United States alone there are dozens of populated places named Bethlehem. So the place name itself does not supply a complete definition of the location, and we may have to add the name of the country and perhaps even of the district.

Secondly, a specific geographical feature may have more than one name. A Dutchman may refer to his country's capital as Den Haag. A foreigner will look up the place in his atlas and find The Hague or s' Gravenhage, and will be unaware that he has indeed hit upon the correct place.

Thirdly, in this age of computers and information technology a quantitative definition of location is indispensable for digital geographical processing, especially in a GIS (geographic information system), including maps, statistics, and indexes such as gazetteers.

Incidentally, the first disadvantage mentioned above in connection with names as locators applies also to the ordinal definition of location by map squares: a single square may include more than one appearance of a specific toponym. This is certainly true of names such as Olifantsfontein or Nooitgedacht in South Africa, which appear dozens and perhaps hundreds of times in the country at large, and (in the case of Nooitgedacht) over a dozen in a single 1:50,000-scale map sheet.

IV. The Geographical Graticule vs. Topographic Grids

It is thus clear that for a precise and unambiguous definition of location of a given toponym a quantitative method is mandatory, but, in cases of homonyms (different places with identical names), perhaps not enough. Such a framework is supplied by the various coordinate systems, with which we shall briefly deal now. No proper national gazetteer of geographical names is complete without reference to the coordinates of each name. Since these coordinates are, in most cases, taken from maps, air photos, or directly from GPS (global positioning systems), we shall below deal with the principles involved.

Geographical coordinates seem to be the most ancient quantitative method of defining location, at least in western literature. The earliest list of geographical names complete with quantitative locators is Ptolemy's *Geographia* of the second century, which records some 8,100 places by their names and with their geographical coordinates. The net of circular lines of latitude on the globe, also called parallels (because their planes are parallel to each other and to that of the equator), and of lines of longitude or meridians (which are half 'great circles' extending from pole to pole), is called the geographical *graticule*. Latitude of a place on the globe (and one should never forget that all toponyms refer to places on a *spheroidal* body) is measured north or south from the equator (lat. 0°) as angles, in degrees, minutes and seconds, and varies between 90°N at the North Pole and 90°S at the South Pole. Longitude is similarly measured as an angle east or west from the prime meridian of Greenwich, England (longitude 0°) and varies between 180°W and 180°E (which coincide, and form the basis of the International Date Line). These measurements thus constitute a precise quantitative system, and its degree of precision is limited only by the smallest unit used (degrees, minutes or seconds and their fractions).

In order to satisfy readers with a proper background in cartography or geodesy it should be mentioned that referring to the Earth as a sphere is only a first approximation. To be precise, the Earth is an irregular body; just go out and look at the nearest mountain and you will see the truth of this statement. But, as a base for more precise calculations of location, as well as for topographic mapping and for specific uses such as computing satellite and missile trajectories, a geometrical shape has to be assumed. On this theoretical surface the mountains, valleys and depressions of the 'real Earth' can then be superimposed. The first approximation thus is the sphere with constant radius R (for our purposes a value of R=6371 km is sufficient). A better approximation is a so-called oblate ellipsoid of rotation, which can be visualized as a sphere slightly flattened at the two poles: the equatorial radius is roughly 6378 km while the polar radius is only some 22 km less or some 6356 km, the flattening ratio thus being approximately 1/300.

Therefore, meridians are not half-circles but near-circular half-ellipses. A further refinement is the so-called geoid used mainly in computing precise altitudes. The surface of this shape is, at all points, perpendicular to the direction of gravity, and can be visualized by imagining the oceans extending below the continents.

So we should speak of the Earth not as a spherical but as a spheroidal body. However, being toponymists and not geodesists we shall continue to use the approximation of the spherical Earth!

In spite of what has been said above concerning the sphericity of the Earth, it is often convenient to deal with only a limited portion of the Earth's surface and regard this at large scale (and therefore in detail) not as curved but as a flat surface, a plane. This is what every conventional topographic map enables one to do. The method of transferring places from the spheroidal surface of the Earth to the plane map sheet is called a cartographic projection. Since the representations of the lines of the graticule in a plane map are curved (except in the so-called normal cylindrical projections), and therefore inconvenient for measuring coordinate values from them, it is common practice to superimpose a plane rectangular net of squares on the map, of the well-known type called Cartesian coordinates, and this is called a topographic or local grid, or, if it covers a national territory, a national grid, the coordinates then being called national coordinates. Most countries have such a national grid, adapted to the particular needs of the country involved. But some grids were designed specifically for inter-national use over wider regions. One example is the grid based on the Gauss-Krüger projection; another, now widely accepted and used around the world, is the UTM system. Such rectangular coordinates are useful for describing the location of names (which in a map does not necessarily coincide with the location of the respective geographical objects), mainly in land areas. In extended sea areas, especially in small-scale maps, where less precision is required, definition by geographical latitude and longitude is often more convenient.

Ⅴ. Placing a Maritime Name

It was said above that a name can define a very large area such as a continent or an ocean. Also it was said that a geographical object must be defined before it can be named. And herein may lie a further problem. In order to correctly describe an object such as a sea, for example, in a map, its outline must be represented indeed as a line, graphic or digitized, that is, converted into a polygon, a closed 'string' of point coordinates. The name can then be inserted at any convenient point within the polygon, for example at the center of gravity of the area. Since the outline of the maritime item, at least in a small-scale map, is usually an objective line, there should not be any difficulty in performing this operation.

But what about a contested sea area? Besides its different territorial waters which are governed by endonyms, it might include secondary areas such as EEZs (extended economic zones) – which may not be recognized by all countries bordering the maritime item under review.[3] It might also have other 'closed' areas. Economical rivalry is perhaps the chief agent for dissention,

---

3) See also Kadmon, Naftali (2007), Endonym or exonym – is there a missing term in maritime names?, *Ninth United Nations Conference on the Standardization of Geographical Names*, E/CONF.98/6, New York.

political rivalry following in second place, this often being connected to security considerations. In most cases of sea areas bordered by more than one national authority, different endonyms are often used by the respective countries, as is the case of the East Sea/Sea of Japan. When those names are applied not only to a country's own territorial waters but to the entire maritime object including territorial waters, strictly speaking they then form exonyms in the languages of the other countries. There remains the case of the open or high seas which do not come under the jurisdiction of any one national authority. Here, any toponym can be applied.

Relevant examples would be the Black Sea or the Baltic Sea (where no toponymic tension seems to exist), or the Persian/Arabian Gulf and the East Sea/Sea of Japan, where it does. In such instances, selecting the location of the appropriate name might depend on the definition of the outline or polygon selected.

And this, again, depends on the scale of the respective map, and will probably change with map scale, undergoing some generalization. In the case of the roughly convex form of the territorial waters of the East Sea, there is no problem in placing the name, and in any but very-small-scale maps inserting the two allonyms.

Finally, the present author always points to the example of the three Scandinavian countries which, by consent, decided on the single name form 'Skagerrak' for this northern maritime item, with its single geographical definition, to replace the three different former name forms. One can only hope that other countries involved in a similar situation but at present still resisting a common solution, would follow suit!

Naftali Kadmon

Emeritus Professor Naftali Kadmon, B.A., M.Sc., Ph.D., has been lecturing on cartography and toponymy at the Hebrew University of Jerusalem for 25 years. Since 1977 and until retiring in 2007 he represented his country at United Nations institutions on geographical names, among others as chairman of UNGEGN's working group on terminology and as editor of the U.N. six-language *Glossary of Terms for the Standardization of Geographical Names*. An author of several books on toponymy in Hebrew, English and Japanese, he still serves as chairman of the Israeli Government Names Commission's Committee on Geographical Names.

Is "Exonym" an Appropriate Term for Names of Features Beyond Any Sovereignty? [1]

Peter Jordan

I. Exonyms: Still Many Open Questions

Although the United Nations Group of Experts on Geographical Names (UNGEGN) has since its foundation made remarkable progress in resolving many problems of standardization and in establishing a practicable terminology, and although exonyms have from the very beginning been in the focus of its discussions, the contents of the terms *exonym* and *endonym* are still not clearly defined and there are still many open questions related to them. One of them is, whether the term exonym covers also features beyond any sovereignty such as international waters.

Naftali Kadmon, at that time the convenor of the UNGEGN Working Group on Toponymic Terminology and the editor of the UNGEGN Glossary of Terms for the Standardization of Geographical Names, has raised this question in his Working Paper submitted to the Ninth United Nations Conference on the

---

1) This paper has been presented at *The 16ᵗʰ International Seminar on Sea Names* (2010).

Standardization of Geographical Names, New York, 21-30 August 2007 (Kadmon 2007a). Roman STANI-FERTL has recently, at the 10th Meeting of the UNGEGN Working Group on Exonyms in Tainach, 28-30 April 2010, urged to put this question on the agenda of the Working Group.

As with many other questions, the new UNGEGN definitions of the *endonym* and the *exonym*[2] do not provide any answer. They have by purpose been formulated in a way that makes them open for various interpretations and have – compared to their predecessors – just the advantage of not being overlapping.

II. Two Contrasting Views

Naftali Kadmon argues in his paper quoted above (Kadmon 2007a), that maritime names in a certain language were endonyms in these parts of a sea, over which a country in which this language is official or well-established exerts some kind of jurisdiction, i.e.

---

2) **Endonym:** Name of a geographical feature in an official or well-established language occurring in that area where the feature is situated. *Examples*: Vārānasī (not Benares); Aachen (not Aix-la-Chapelle); Krung Thep (not Bangkok); Al-Uqṣur (not Luxor).

Exonym: Name used in a specific language for a geographical feature situated outside the area where that language is widely spoken, and differing in its form from the respective endonym(s) in the area where the geographical feature is situated. *Examples*: Warsaw is the English exonym for Warszawa (Polish); Mailand is German for Milano; Londres is French for London; Kūlūniyā is Arabic for Köln. The officially romanized endonym Moskva for Москва is not an exonym, nor is the Pinyin form Beijing, while Peking is an exonym. The United Nations recommends minimizing the use of exonyms in international usage (Kadmon 2007b, p. 2).

its territorial waters. Names in languages not corresponding to the requirements of being official or well-established in this country will be termed *exonyms*.

He exemplifies this by the Korean and Japanese names for the Sea of Japan/East Sea (see fig. 1): The Korean name Donghae (Tong Hae) has the terminological status of an endonym in the territorial waters of Korea and acquires the status of an exonym in the territorial waters of Japan, while the Japanese name Nihon Kai has the terminological status of an endonym in the territorial waters of Japan and becomes an exonym in the territorial waters of Korea.

Outside territorial waters, according to Kadmon, both names have neither the terminological status of an endonym nor of an exonym, they are just *allonyms*. For Kadmon it "follows that there is a need for a new term to be added to the Glossary of Terms for the Standardization of Geographical Names, namely the status of a toponym for a maritime feature in international waters." (Kadmon 2007a, p. 4).

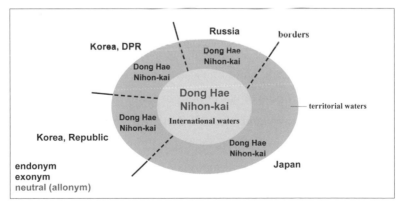

<Figure 1> Kadmon's view applied to Sea of Japan/East Sea

In my opinion, this is a premature conclusion and it is also not sufficiently explained. Why can the Korean name Donghae (Tong hae) acquire exonym status only in the territorial waters of another country, e.g. Japan? Why not also with reference to international waters? Does the acquisition of an exonym status require the existence of an endonym as a counterpart?

While I am fully in line with Kadmon's view that a geographical name for a transboundary feature can change its terminological status according to the portion of the feature to which it is applied, I would – in contrast to him – express the opinion that a name can also have exonym status, where the counterpart of an endonym is missing, e.g., with reference to international waters. I will explain this argument in more detail later.

Paul Woodman has in several papers (a.o. Woodman 2009a, b) expressed a view quite different from Kadmon's. His basic concept is that one name in one language for one feature cannot change in terminological status, cannot simultaneously be an endonym and an exonym. According to him (see fig. 2) the Korean name Donghae (Tong hae) is an endonym all over the feature, i.e. in the territorial waters of Korea as well as Japan, but also with reference to international waters. The same is, of course, true *vice versa*: The Japanese name *Nihon Kai* has endonym status all over the Sea, no matter, which country and where it exerts jurisdiction.

This resolves our problem (Is there a need for a third term besides *endonym* and *exonym* for international waters?) in a most comfortable way: There is no need for a third term, since all languages official or well-established in the coastal countries of a sea are

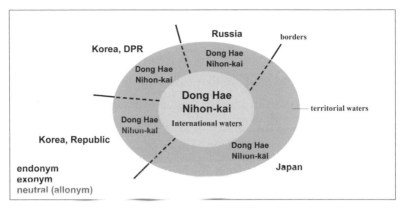

<Figure 2> Woodman's view applied to Sea of Japan/East Sea

endonyms all over the feature. Names in languages not official or not well-established in coastal countries like the English names SeaofJapan/EastSeainourcase,have,ofcourse,thestatusofexonyms, since there is everywhere the counterpart of an endonym, even in international waters, in areas beyond any national sovereignty.

Paul's strongest argument for his view, that a name remains an endonym also outside the territorial waters of a certain country, is, that a feature is indivisible in emotional terms. The emotional affection of a certain linguistic community to the feature, e.g., a sea, cannot be divided into zones (territorial waters, international waters, territorial waters of another country), but refers to the feature as a whole and to all its parts.

Sungjae Choo (Choo 2009) as well as the author of this paper (Jordan 2009a, b) have replied that people develop emotional ties rather to places in the sense of Tuan (Tuan 1977) than to the entirety of geographical features, which are always constructs and in fact abstract spatial entities. This is especially true for large natural features like seas, mountain ranges or streams. Affection of coastal dwellers to a sea, e.g., fades away when they leave the place where they live more or less as a function of distance. They are anyway unlikely to claim that coasts far beyond their horizon (inhabited by speakers of another language having their own name for the sea) were to the same extent 'theirs' as the coast and the part of the sea they can watch from their houses, where they go for a swim and which is navigated by local fisher boats.

It is not the place here to mention also other arguments in this respect (cf. Jordan 2009a, b), since our current question is a different one.

Ⅲ. Proposing a Synthesis

While I share Paul Woodman's opinion that there should be nothing besides the endonym/exonym divide and I would strongly support Naftali Kadmon's view that the endonym status of a name for a transboundary feature is to be confined to places, where a certain language is official or well-established as well as to territorial waters of countries, in which this is the case, I cannot follow him, when he implicitly concludes that the term *exonym* cannot apply to names for international waters, since they lack the counterpart of an endonym.

Must there be a counterpart? Does our new definition of the exonym require a counterpart? Yes, perhaps. It says that an exonym is a name "differing in its form from the respective endonym(s) in the area where the geographical feature is situated." (Kadmon 2007b, p. 3) This may indeed be interpreted as hinting at an endonym as a requirement for an exonym. But it may also be interpreted in the opposite way: If there is an endonym, the exonym must differ in its form.

Applied to the Sea of Japan/East Sea this synthesis would result in what is represented by fig. 3: The Korean and Japanese names, resp., have endonym status in the waters under the jurisdiction of their countries. Outside, also in international waters, they assume the status of exonyms.

International waters are, by the way, not the only features without a corresponding endonym. There are lots of historical features lacking an adequate current endonym: *Byzantine Empire, Ottoman Empire, Habsburg Empire, Moesia, Tauria, Noricum, Troy*, etc.[3]

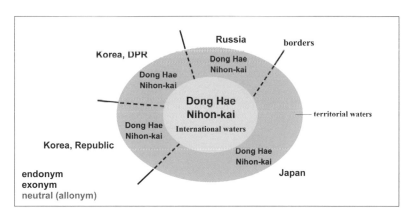

<Figure 3> Synthesis applied to Sea of Japan/East Sea

---

3) They mostly had a historical contemporary endonym. In some cases the current exonym was the historical endonym (Noricum, Moesia).

Are they all something besides the endonym/exonym divide? Must we find even a fourth term for them?

I do not think so, since they all coincide very well with the basic concept of the exonym, i.e. to be a name from without, a name used by a linguistic community <u>not</u> inhabiting the place in question. Whether the place is inhabited by an endonym community or not or is under the jurisdiction of an endonym community is a different question, which does not matter in our context. It would only matter, when it comes to define, whether a name is an endonym or not.

Peter Jordan

Peter Jordan has served as, Honorary and Associate Professor, cultural geographer and atlas editor at the Austrian Academy of Sciences, chairman of the Austrian Board on Geographical Names, convenor in charge of the UNGEGN Working Group on Exonyms.

REFERENCES

Choo, Sungjae (2009), Geographical feature and endonym: the case of East Sea/Sea of Japan. *The 15th International Seminar on Sea Names*, 3-5 September 2009, Sydney, Australia.

Jordan, Peter (2009a), What is an endonym? Still a question after decades of standardization. United Nations Group of Experts on Geographical Names, 25th Session, Nairobi, 5-12 May 2009, WP 32.

Jordan, Peter (2009b), The endonym/exonym divide related to transboundary features: Recent discussions in the UNGEGN Working Group on Exonyms. *The 15th International Seminar on Sea Names*, 3-5 September 2009, Sydney, Australia.

Kadmon, Naftali (2007a), Endonym or Exonym – is there a Missing Term in Maritime Names? Ninth United Nations Conference on the Standardization of Geographical Names, New York, 21–30 August 2007. United Nations, New York, E/CONF.98/ 6/ Add.1.

Kadmon, Naftali (2007b), *Glossary of Terms for the Standardization of Geographical Names*, Addendum. United Nations, New York, ST/ESA/STAT/SER.M/85/Add.1.

Tuan, Yi-Fu (1977), Space and place: The perspective of experience. Minneapolis: University of Minnesota Press.

Woodman, Paul (2009a), The Nature of the Endonym. United Nations Group of Experts on Geographical Names, 25th Session, Nairobi, 5-12 May 2009, WP 1.

Woodman, Paul (2009b), The Sea of the Three Endonyms. *The 15th International Seminar on Sea Names*, 3-5 September 2009, Sydney, Australia.

Bilingual and Multilingual Marine and Lacustrine Names: Consent and Dissent [1]

Naftali Kadmon

As background to the discussions revolving around the names Donghae and Sea of Japan, and perhaps as a guide in future cases of a similar nature, this paper deals with a brief analysis of bilingual or multilingual names applied to open seas or inland seas, that is, large lakes – names which have been subject to international tension or given rise to international problems. Only in very few cases has there been international intervention toward a toponymic settlement of the problem, and then with little success. The cases, each represented by just a few examples, are sorted roughly according to the severity of the toponymic problem, as follows:

> unification by official consent or by mute assent;
> bilingual or multilingual names by consent as endonyms;
> uncontested 'exonymic' names conferred, for example, by explorers or travelers;
> politically - induced name changes;
> toponymic - maritime conflict or political rivalry.

---

1) This paper has been presented at *The 10th International Seminar on the Naming of Seas* (2004).

The terminology employed here conforms to that prescribed by the United Nations *Glossary of Terms for the Standardization of Geographical Names*. [1] It should be noted that while 'maritime name' has been defined (as term No. 221) in the first edition (2002), the term 'lacustrine name' was included in the Addendum of 30 August 2007 as term No. 218/a, 'name of a lake or of an inland sea'.

In effect, we are dealing here with a matter of standardization, and mostly with cases involving two or more countries. The overriding (but hardly attainable) aim is the 'one object – one name' principle.

But while national standardization of geographical names can be imposed by a national authority, such as a government-installed board of geographical names, true international standardization can be attained only by cooperation and goodwill. If such goodwill cannot be achieved, there remains another means of obtaining *de facto*, if not *de jure*, recognition of allonyms by the international community. This, in certain instances, is mapping, and will be briefly dealt with in the final paragraph of this paper.

I. Unification by Official Consent or by Mute Assent

Perhaps the best example of cooperation between countries – although involving only the unification of the spelling of a name – is the name of the sea arm between southern Sweden and Norway and northern Denmark. This was spelled respectively Skagerak,

Skagerack, and Skagerrak by the three countries until, in 1970, they agreed on the uniform and standardized name Skagerrak, now used by all three.

A different case is that of the lowest water body on Earth, sharing its lacustrine surface – at the (rapidly falling) elevation of, today, some 425 meters below Mediterranean mean sea level (m.s.l.) between Israel and the Hashemite Kingdom of Jordan. The former calls it *Yam haMelaḥ*, המלח ים, (pronounced Yam Hamelach), The Salt Sea, while the latter's name for it is *al-Baḥr al-Mayyit*, آلبحر آلميت, The Dead Sea, and also *Baḥr Lut*, بحر لوط, Sea of Lot. But since this is an internationally well-known geographical feature, both countries use the same English exonym for it, namely Dead Sea, used also in translation into nearly all other languages. The specific component, 'dead', points to the fact that owing to the extremely high salt content of its water, some 33 percent by weight, it admits no living organism.

II. Bilingual or Multilingual Names by Consent or by Mute Assent

The English Channel can here serve as a first example. Its French name is *la Manche*, that is, the sleeve (and this, as an exonym, is also its German name, *Ärmelkanal*). Both English Channel and la Manche are endonyms, and no country challenges the other concerning its use.

Another example, not very far from the first, is the sea which extends between Germany in the South, the eastern counties of

England in the West and Danish Jylland (English exonym Jutland) in the East. All three countries apply wind-rose names to it – but different ones. Germany, naturally, calls it *Nordsee*, while England uses the same name in English, *North Sea*, although it lies to the north only of the county of Norfolk. Denmark, to the east, names it *Vesterhavet*, the Western Sea. Here we find diversity by consent.

Between Sweden, Germany, Poland, the Baltic States, and Russia is the Baltic Sea. This English exonym represents, among others, the Swedish name *Östsjön* (East Bay), the German one *Ostsee*, the Russian *Балтийкое море* and the Estonian one *Läänemeri*. Again, no problem is involved.

The sea which stretches between Greece in the West and Turkey in the east carries the name *Aegean* since Greek antiquity. But in the first Turkish atlas printed in Turkey in 1803 this sea was named Anatolian, after the name of the west Asian peninsula of *Anatolia*, known in history also as Asia Minor, which constituted the major part of Turkey. Kemal Atatürk used the name *Akdeniz* (Mediterranean Sea) for the Aegean. The present-day official Turkish name for it is *Ege Denizi*.

As a final example let us take the Red Sea. Its Arabic name is *al-Bahr al-Ahmar*, البحرآلأحمر, (pronounced al-Bachr al-Achmar, with the ch roughly as in German 'ach' or Scottish 'loch'), meaning indeed the red sea, translated from ancient Greek texts and maps Ἐρυθρά Θάλασσα and from Latin ones *Ruber Mare*, or *Mare Rubrum*. However Israel, which governs just a small stretch of shore of the Red Sea in the Gulf of Aqaba or Gulf of Eilat, names it in Hebrew *Yam Suf*, ים סוּף, meaning reed sea, after the reeds which grow along its shores–and this is its original biblical name.

Ⅲ. Uncontested 'Exonymic' Names Conferred, for Example, by Explorers or Travelers

Here we are dealing with toponyms whose language differs from the official language or languages of the surrounding country.

Beagle is the English name of a species of dog. *Canal Beagle* is the maritime name of the narrow waterway between Spanish-speaking southern Argentina's Tierra del Fuego and Chile's XIIth Region in the North, and Chilean Isla de Navarino and the Cape Horn (Cabo de Hornos) area in the South. The name commemorates Charles Darwin's ship of this name which traversed it in 1832. The English specific component Beagle has been accepted as part of the official name in a Spanish-speaking region.

Estrecho Wellington, Estrecho Nelson, and *Canal Baker* are three waterways between the mainland of southern Chile's XIth Region and the archipelago of a multitude of islands sheltering it in the west. These names, with purely English specific components were accepted by the purely Spanish-speaking government of Chile as valid endonyms and appear thus in Chilean maps and gazetteers.

Ⅳ. Politically-induced Name Changes

This part of the paper deals primarily with changes of names of large lakes resulting from changes in the political environment. Toponymic history reveals several major periods of 'revolutionary' name changing. One of these, and the one with which we shall be dealing shortly, occurred after the end of, or even during the course of, World War II. Numerous countries threw off the yoke of their colonial masters, declared their independence and chose new names not only for their newly acquired territory but also for topographic features within it, including lakes, especially if their national language did not coincide with that of the former colonial power. In many such cases the new government simply reverted to former endemic endonyms. These had often been kept alive in the local language.

One such case was the *Sea of Galilee*, also known in English as *Lake Genezareth*, in British-administered Palestine which in 1948 became the State of Israel. It re-acquired its old Hebrew lacustrine name, ים כנרת, *Yam Kinneret*, that is, Sea of Kinneret, as the official toponym, documented already some 2,500 years ago in the Hebrew Bible (the 'Old Testament') in the fourth Book of Moses (Num. 34,11), attesting to its antiquity. In the King James ('Authorised') English translation it is found as Chinnereth.

Some African examples are *Lake Nyasa* in British-held Nyasaland which became *Lake Malawi*, or *Lake Rudolf* in British Kenya which became *Lake Turkana* in the Republic of Kenya. But *Lake Victoria*, shared by Kenya, Uganda, and Tanzania, retained its imperial name. *Lake Edward* in Uganda and in the Democratic Republic of the Congo was, from 1976 to 1979, given the name *Lake Idi Amin Dada*. Guess by whom......

An interesting case is found in the open sea constituting the eastern border of Kenya and Tanzania. This is part of the Indian Ocean. But in older maps, such as the pre-World War II Times atlases, one finds the name *Azanian Sea*, which surrounds the Zanzibar Islands. This maritime name rather disappeared later, but its origin is of interest. In the middle of the twelfth century the Arab geographer and cartographer Idrisi of Ceuta entered the name Ard az-Zanj in his maps in parts of eastern Africa. The translation of this Arabic name is Land of the Blacks, or the 'niggers', and was apparently given by Arab traders from the Arabian Peninsula who frequently crossed the Red Sea pursuing the slave trade, 'exporting' thousands of black Africans. Az-Zanj later turned into Azania, and is in effect a derogatory allonym of Africa.

V . Toponymic-maritime Conflict or Political Rivalry

We now come to the more severe form of relations between maritime allonyms, or rather between their proponents. The fact – well known to many toponymists – that a geographical name can lead to warfare, actual physical warfare and not only verbal, has been described in the book *Toponymy: The Lore, Laws and Language of Geographical Names* [2] with the help of the example of Macedonia. This name nearly led to a real – and not just toponymic–war between Greece and the Former Yugoslav Republic of Macedonia. So the United Nations assigned to the new republic the official name FYROM, an acronym of the final part of the previous sentence. But in the present paper we are dealing with maritime names.

In 1991 there began the first Gulf War. Which gulf? This war did not start because of a name, but two allonyms of the same maritime object featured prominently in it and in the original reports of the belligerents and of some other parties involved. The people in the country to its east call it the *Persian Gulf*, and so do most western countries, following the ancient Greeks and Ptolemy. But not so the inhabitants of the Arab countries bordering the Gulf on the western side; for them it is the *Arabian Gulf*, al-Khalij al-ʿArabi, الخليج العربي. These differences even spill over into the economic sphere. A well-known British cartographic firm produced, in 1977, two versions of a map of this same Gulf, differing only in these and a few other names, thus ensuring sales to both sides, and making everybody happy – perhaps most of all the firm itself. Lately a demand has been raised for conferring the Arabic name *Arabian Gulf* as an official one in all maps and atlases.

And this brings to mind the case of Donghae, the East Sea or Sea of Korea, and the refusal of Japan to recognize this allonym of the Sea of Japan. However, today many cartographic institutions around the world do already insert both names in their maps.

I shall close with a last case, involving the Mediterranean Sea, which occurred in the last century. Italy, under the dictator Benito Mussolini, insisted on the name *Mare Nostrum* ('our sea') because the Mediterranean ('between the lands') lay between the Italian mainland and its colonies in North Africa. But World War II quickly relegated this name *ad acta historicae*, since it was, indeed, a latter-day revival of an old Roman name, now to be used no more.

VI. The Formal Status of Maritime Names

Let us briefly investigate the formal status of the names we have been dealing with above. This depends on two factors, namely (a) what use is made of a name, and (b) to which part of the sea or of a lake the name is applied.

As to (a), a remark must be made regarding the context in which the name is used. There is a difference between two uses of a toponym. On the one hand it may be used in an international application such as a map or any other document designed for international use or circulation. On the other hand it may appear in a text in a particular language which is not that of the country of the specific name in question. For the former applications the United Nations Conferences on the Standardization of Geographical Names recommend (they cannot prescribe or force) to use official endonyms when referring to places 'abroad', that is, where the language differs from that of the map or atlas. Therefore in an English atlas the capital of Poland should appear as Warszawa (and not as Warsaw), København (and not Copenhagen), or Athina (and not Athens). But in the second case, for 'home' or 'domestic' use, and in particular in general literature and running texts, exonyms can still be used, for example, in the forms in parentheses in the previous sentence. But the United Nations warn against the excessive use of exonyms because they might give rise to international friction and even conflict.

Now to point (b). There is clearly no difference of opinion on the status of a name of a lake or of an inland sea entirely enclosed within a single state. Only this country can decide on the name, which then becomes the official endonym. The same can be said of the territorial waters of a particular state. Thus, *Gulf of Aqaba* (Jordan, Saudi Arabia, and Egypt) and *Gulf of Elat* (Israel) are both valid endonyms. The same is true of a lake or inland sea which shares its shoreline among two or more states, such as the *Dead Sea* (Israel and Jordan).

But what about the sea areas outside the territorial waters of large water bodies such as oceans and their parts? Here, no official exclusive endonym can be applied to the entire sea. Therefore any country, whether bordering on the sea in question or not, can apply its own names. Examples are the *Baltic Sea* mentioned above, or the *Pacific Ocean/Stiller Ozean*, or *Ishavet/Nördliches Eismeer/ СЕВЕРНЫЙ ЛЕДОВИЫЙ ОКЕАН*. Formally, of course, one should not infringe on the official names of territorial waters, though practically this is sometimes unavoidable, especially in small-scale maps. Often such 'nationally based' names of parts of a sea extend over the entire water body.

This also seems to cover the case of the sea between the Korean peninsula and the Japanese archipelago, where both the Japanese name Nihon Kai (Sea of Japan) and the Korean name Donghae (East Sea) can both be equally applied.

VII. So, Finally, What Can be Done in a Case of Conflict?

The first thing to do in a case of different names being applied to a single water body and leading to friction would be to follow the recommendations of the United Nations, namely for the two (or more) countries to try to reach agreement on a single unified name–as in the case of the Skagerrak cited above. If different allonyms still prevail without giving rise to toponymic or politi cal problems, as in the case of bilingual and multilingual names described above, perhaps no action needs to be taken.

However, if one side in a names conflict feels it needs redress from the other, it can turn to a third party in order to try and solve the problem. The United Nations would be a natural third party in such a case. But as has already been noted, the world organization, through the U.N. Conferences on the Standardization of Geographical Names, has no powers to force a solution on the sides. This can be done only by the Security Council or the General Assembly and has been attempted to the present writer's knowledge only once (and not very successfully), in the case of Greece vs. Macedonia/FYROM.

But if this does not help, a practical step can still be tried. Since maps and atlases are perhaps the major and most important repository of geographical names, even in this age of digital geographic information systems (GIS), the party which feels slighted or underprivileged can approach map and atlas publishers around the world with the request to print its preferred maritime name in addition to any other. If this request is reasonable, and is accompanied by documentary evidence supporting the claim, it might be followed up by cartographers (and perhaps by other publishers). In a map there is, however, one limitation: the scale of the map may be too small for including more than one name. In this case, it is up to the cartographer – or to his national authorities – to decide which name to insert.

Thus, the present paper still ends on a note of 'active indecision' or 'indecisive action', but with the hope that in future, cases of this nature will be resolved by agreement and consent.

Notes:

[1] United Nations (2002), *Glossary of Terms for the Standardization of Geographical Names*, ed. Naftali Kadmon. New York: United Nations Publications.

[2] Naftali Kadmon (2001), *Toponymy: The Lore, Laws and Language of Geographical Names*. New York: Vantage Press.

Naftali Kadmon

Emeritus Professor Naftali Kadmon, B.A., M.Sc., Ph.D., has been lecturing on cartography and toponymy at the Hebrew University of Jerusalem for 25 years. Since 1977 and until retiring in 2007 he represented his country at United Nations institutions on geographical names, among others as chairman of UNGEGN's working group on terminology and as editor of the U.N. six-language *Glossary of Terms for the Standardization of Geographical Names*. An author of several books on toponymy in Hebrew, English and Japanese, he still serves as chairman of the Israeli Government Names Commission's Committee on Geographical Names.

Use of National Names for International Bodies of Water [1]

Alexander B. Murphy

Over the past two decades, the study of the history of cartography has undergone a significant transformation. Traditionally, maps were treated as objective representations of reality, and studies in the history of cartography emphasized the development of different approaches to rendering the spatial organization of the world in maps.

Beginning in the 1980s, a growing number of commentators argued that a real understanding of maps and mapmaking had to be premised on the recognition that maps are not neutral, value-free representations. Such arguments paved the way for new research agendas centered on the ideological underpinnings of cartographic undertakings. In the process, maps began to be seen as windows into political and social worlds, revealing the ideas and prejudices of the social contexts out of which they arose.

Efforts to contextualize cartographic representations led scholars to investigate a variety of matters related to the production and construction of maps. Attention was focused on why maps were

---

1) This paper has been presented at *The 11ᵗʰ International Seminar on The Naming of Seas* (2005).

made of some places but not of others, why certain features of the landscape were singled out for emphasis, and how particular cartographic design elements were used to make specific social and political points. Yet for all the attention to different facets of map making, the actual naming of places on maps has received little attention. This is surprising given that the rendering of place names on maps can be an important way in which political statements are made and ideologies are reproduced.

I . Naming International Seas after Nations or States

There are many different names attached to international bodies of water around the world, and most of these cause little problem. However, when an international body of water bears the name of a nation or state, the potential for conflict arises. This is because of the extraordinary importance of the modern territorial state system in the perceptual and functional ordering of human affairs. Yet the use of national names for international bodies of water is a relatively common practice.

There are twenty-seven prominent cases in which a commonly used name for an international body of water is either (1) the name of a current independent country, (2) the name of the dominant national group in a currently independent country, or (3) the name of a national group/region that has actively sought independence during the latter part of the twentieth century. The relevant cases are as follows:

Arabian Sea	Bay of Biscay	Bight of Benin
Bight of Biafra	Denmark Strait	East China Sea
English Channel	Gulf of Finland	Gulf of Guinea
Gulf of Honduras	Gulf of Mexico	Gulf of Oman
Gulf of Panama	Gulf of Thailand	Gulf of Venezuela
Irish Sea	Korea Bay	Korea Strait
Mozambique Channel	Norwegian Sea	Persian Gulf/Arabian Gulf
Philippine Sea	East Sea/Sea of Japan	Singapore Strait
South China Sea/East Sea	Taiwan Strait	Timor Sea

As this list reveals, there are international bodies of water bearing the names of states or nations in many parts of the world. Moreover, there is much diversity in the circumstances surrounding the adoption of those names. Some of the names have been in use for long periods of time (e.g, Persian Gulf), whereas others are relatively recent adoptions (e.g., Sea of Japan).

II. Factors Affecting Contentiousness

Research on levels of controversy surrounding the use of national names for international bodies of water suggests that some cases are much more contentious than others:

High Degree of Contention (Efforts to oppose current naming practices)
Persian Gulf   East Sea/Sea of Japan

South China Sea

Moderate Degree of Contention (Different renderings on maps but little effort to oppose current naming practices)

Bay of Biscay	English Channel
Gulf of Thailand	

Low Degree of Contention (Little evidence of concern over current naming practices)

Bight of Benin	Bight of Biafra
Denmark Strait	East China Sea
Gulf of Finland	Gulf of Guinea
Gulf of Honduras	Gulf of Mexico
Gulf of Oman	Gulf of Panama
Irish Sea	Korea Bay
Korea Strait	Mozambique Channel
Norwegian Sea	Philippine Sea
Singapore Strait	Taiwan Strait
Timor Sea	

Insufficient Evidence to Assess (Insufficient evidence available to allow for a systematic assessment of the case)

Arabian Sea	Gulf of Venezuela

Although there is some inevitable subjectivity in the grouping of cases into these categories, they provide a useful starting point for considering the circumstances that may produce differing levels of confrontation over the use of national names for international bodies of water. The following circumstances appear to be of particular relevance:

A. Circumstances present in highly contentious cases:
  1. A name commonly used for the body of water is the name of a state with a recent history of political or economic hegemony in the region (Persian/Arabian Gulf; East Sea/Sea of Japan; South China Sea/East Sea).
B. Circumstance present in moderately contentious cases
  1. There is a long history of conflict between two of the states bordering the sea (English Channel; Gulf of Thailand).
  2. The name of the sea raises issues that concern the territorial integrity of interested states (Bay of Biscay).
C. Circumstances present in relatively non-contentious cases
  1. Only one state has a significant border on the sea (Denmark Strait; Gulf of Panama; Philippine Sea; Norwegian Sea).
  2. The sea bears the name of a nation with no hegemonic potential in the region (Bight of Benin; Bight of Biafra; Gulf of Guinea; Gulf of Oman; Irish Sea; Timor Sea).
  3. The sea bears the name of a state with no history of hegemonic dominance in the region (Gulf of Honduras; Gulf of Mexico; Korea Bay; Korea Strait; Mozambique Channel; Singapore Strait).

4. There are special geopolitical considerations at play that
   work against controversy
   a. Gulf of Finland – Estonia's historic ethno-cultural ties to
      Finland and its need for Finnish support
   b. East China Sea – Japan and Korea's concern not to upset
      power balances and undermine a name reflecting the United
      Kingdom's presence in Hong Kong
   c. Taiwan Strait – China's concern to show that Taiwan is
      not an independent country

As these circumstances suggest, the geopolitical and geo-historical
context affects levels of contoversy over the use of national
names for international bodies of water. Most obviously, every one
of the highly contentious cases shares a geopolitical commonality
arising out of differential power relations, and the moderately
contentious cases seem to occur where at least some historical
territorial issues can be identified. Most of the uncontested cases
arise in circumstances where either no other state has a significant
interest in the naming issue or where the name that is attached to
the international body of water is that of a state that has not been
a historic threat to others in the region – and is unlikely to become
such a threat in the foreseeable future.

III. Implications for Current and Prospective Controversies

Geopolitical and geo-historical circumstances are clearly of great relevance to the development of controversy over the use of national names for international bodies of water. The cases where controversy is most likely to develop are in situations where shifting power relations among interested states produce concerns about the hegemonic ambitions of the state after which the international body of water is named. To use an example for illustrative purposes only, if Mozambique were interested in, and able to, assert a growing level of economic and political dominance over Madagascar, the currently benign situation surrounding the naming of the Mozambique Channel might well change.

A more complicated set of implications must be considered in the case of currently active controversies. As we have seen, each of these arises in a situation where unequal power relations have been at play for some time. In a case such as the dispute over the naming of the East Sea/Sea of Japan, differential power relations clearly play a critical role in generating controversy, confirming that naming international bodies of water after nations or states can produce problems where power differences exist now, or have existed in the past. Moving beyond such controversies is clearly difficult, as both sides are likely to see the issue as one that touches on national self-determination. Yet it is impossible to confront such controversies if the concerns of the involved parties are not acknowledged. It follows that, in cases where a commonly used national name is in use, mapmakers, academics, and policy makers should be attuned to the potential for controversy and should be open to the use of alternative names.

Alexander B. Murphy

Alexander B. Murphy is a professor of geography at the
University of Oregon and is also Rippey chair in Liberal
Arts and Sciences. He is a former president of the
Association of American Geographers and senior vice
president of the American Geographical Society.

The Status Quo

East Sea / Sea of Japan:
What is the Problem?

Li Jin-mieung

The East Sea / Sea of Japan has a surface of 978,000 square kilometers, a maximum depth of 3,742 meters, and an average depth of 1,752 m. This sea is a relatively wide and expansive sea bordered by Korea, Japan and Russia which stretches for about 1,100 km from Wonsanman Bay in the west to Hokkaido in the east and for about 1,700 km from the Korea Strait in the south to the Tartar Strait in the north.

The sea is connected with the East China Sea and the Pacific Ocean via the Korea Strait in the southwest, the Pacific Ocean in the east via the Tsugaru Strait which divides Honshu and Hokkaido, and the Sea of Okhotsk by both the La Pérouse (or Soya) Strait which separates Hokkaido from the Russian islands of Sakhalin and the Tartary Strait which separates Sakhalin from the eastern coast of Siberia. Without these four narrow channels, the sea would be an enclosed sea surrounded by land.

The 'Sea of Japan', – the East Sea (1,030,000 m^2) – , is defined by the International Hydrographic Organization as comprising of the waters between the southern coast of the Korean Peninsula to

Jeju Island, waters known as the South Sea in Korea, the Korea Strait (Busan in Korea to Fukuoka in Japan), and extends to the Northern extremity of the Tartary Strait.

This sea has a total coastal length of 6,000 km of which 47 percent belongs to Russia, 36 percent to Japan and 16 percent to Korea. The sea offers a common space between four bordering countries: North Korea with 25 million inhabitants, South Korea 50 million, Japan 128 million and Russia 145 million. The population who live directly on the border of this sea account for roughly 12 million of the inhabitants of the south and east coasts of the Korean Peninsula, 10 million for the north and west coasts of the Japanese archipelago, and several millions for the Russian coasts on two sides of the Gulf of Tartary.

The four bordering countries each have their own territorial waters (22 kilometers from the coast), adjacent zone (44 kilometers), exclusive economic zone (EEZ, 370 kilometers), with the remaining portion being international waters. These four categories of maritime zone were defined by the Montego Bay (Jamaica) Convention of the United Nations on the Right of the Sea in 1982. South Korea and Japan are members of the convention.

The bordering countries have strategic and economic interests, as well as sharing the common responsibility for the sea.

In this sense, the name of the sea is very important. It must be used by everyone concerned.

A sea name, like any geographical place name, serves as a reference point. This is the reason why it is natural that a sea take the name frequently and commonly used by the inhabitants of the area.

Lee Ki-suk, a professor emeritus of geography at Seoul National

University, former president of the East Sea Society and a member of the Academy of Sciences, said, "It is well-known that it took several centuries to correct a monumental collection of incorrect toponyms (geographical place names) in Ptolemy's Atlas. [......] Everyone needs a place name to communicate with others, and then this place name becomes a key element for socio-economical activities, such as cartography, population census, pastimes and leisure activities, postal services, trading activities, etc. "

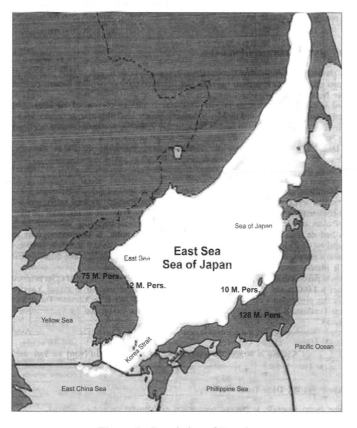

<Figure 1> Population of Donghae

Yu Woo-ik, former professor of geography at Seoul National University, Korean ambassador in China and general secretary of the International Geographical Congress, expressed the same observation in August 2000: "A toponym implies a name given to a place by those whom it belongs to or by those who make use of it, or else by those who are merely concerned."

"Naming a place is the same as assuming possession over it. Or, trying to do so. A seemingly neutral toponym is actually a high-stakes issue, the stakes increase when there is a dispute over a geographical space among several parties", wrote Philippe Pelletier, professor of geography at the Lumière University, in Lyon, France.

The toponyms are carried, diffused and fixed through geographical maps and atlases.

Ⅰ. East Sea / Sea of Japan

In this sense, the problem posed is that the sea between Korea and Japan bears the name 'Sea of Japan', used in the outside world, but unknown by Koreans directly concerned.

The name 'Donghae' (East Sea) is unknown to the Japanese, and 'Nihon-kai' (Sea of Japan) unknown to Koreans. Both 'Donghae / Nihon-kai' need to be used for the persons involved to grasp which sea is quoted, and this until everybody involved in the matter has agreed upon a neutral and pretty name, symbolizing the geographical nature as well as the human surroundings of the sea in question.

Furthermore, the name 'Sea of Japan' has a connotation implying that the sea 'belongs to' Japan or the sea is the 'property' of Japan. Koreans feel frustrated and indignant when they discover the name 'Sea of Japan' on foreign maps for the sea they call Donghae (East Sea).

The two Koreas joined the U.N. in 1991. In 1992, South Korea participated in the U.N. Conference on Standardization of Geographical Names for the first time. On that occasion, the Korean delegation claimed the name East Sea, used since antiquity in Korea, for the sea known as the Sea of Japan. The name is something that Koreans can not easily accept because of the memory of Japanese colonization of their country (1910-1945). Koreans think the sea name relates to their dignity, honor and pride. It's also a question of affirmation of their national identity in the international community.

Koreans see the name Sea of Japan as a historical injustice because the toponym was confirmed by the IHO in 1929 when Korea was a colony of Japan. South Korea became a member of the IHO in 1957, and sent its delegation for the first time in 1962.

The IHO established the document entitled *Limits of the Oceans & Seas* (S-23), an international reference for hydrography. The third version of S-23 is under revision. South Korea argued in 1994 for the inscription of the East Sea beside the Sea of Japan in this document. On Aug. 15, 2002, the IHO sent its proposal of S-23 for the vote of the 72 member countries. In the draft, the page corresponding to the sea between Korea and Japan rested blank. It signified that the name Sea of Japan was dropped down. South Korea expressed its relative satisfaction, while Japan was surprised. Japan acted rapidly and succeeded in getting the IHO to drop the draft.

Japan is determined to defend the name 'Sea of Japan'. The question of naming this sea is a major diplomatic issue between Korea and Japan, toward international communities (U.N. and IHO), geographers, cartographers, editors, and mass media of the third countries.

II. Local Name Is Favored by International Organizations

The name 'Donghae' (East Sea / Mer de l'Est) is the only endonym – local name – for the sea between Korea and Japan that was definitely established in the Korean Peninsula since antiquity, and is still used today. The East Sea is, in this sense, an inalienable item of Korean cultural heritage. But this name has not yet sufficiently acquired usage abroad because people there have been unaware of it until now. Koreans are also responsible for this situation by their ignorance of the matters on the international scene until the beginning of 1990s.

But it's not too late to recognize this historically proven evidence, and repair the error of history, and begin to adopt the double name East Sea / Sea of Japan.

The Japanese adopted the name 'Sea of Japan' (Nihonkai / Mer du Japon), used on the Western maps widely since the beginning of the 19th century. These maps were introduced after the Meiji Restoration in 1868. This means that Sea of Japan is an exonym (foreign name) of Western origin, adopted and rapidly appropriated by Japanese. For this reason, the Sea of Japan doesn't appear in any ancient Japanese document prior to the mid-19th century.

It's only common sense that international communities use East Sea beside Sea of Japan so that Koreans can understand the location relevant to multiple purposes: Navigation of warships and merchant ships, maritime accidents, fishing, leisure, natural resources, protection of the environment and meteorology, and so on.

III. Desirable Toponym

A place name in a country can be revised by the national commission on standardization of geographical names.
Traditionally, the name of seas, gulfs and mountains broaching several countries is fixed by frequency of use, by custom and tradition. Nowadays, an international geographical name is defined, adopted or recommended by the international organizations such as the IHO for the limits and the name of seas and oceans, and by the U.N. Conference of Standardization of Geographical Names for general toponyms. For these international organizations, the problem is not so simple to resolve if there are several names for one geographical space, defended by several countries. For this

purpose, the international authorities have recommendations.

The IHO's resolution of 1974 recommends that the name forms of each of the languages in question should be accepted for charts and publications unless technical reasons prevent this practice on small scale charts; e.g., English Channel / La Manche. The legitimacy of the place or sea name can be contested if it is acquired by a decision taken unilaterally, if it is not founded on the common accord between the parties directly concerned, or if it is not based on the historically and scientifically irrefutable proofs issued from the facts of the involved countries, not from a third party. In this case, a contested name such as Sea of Japan can bear some tension between the protagonist countries.

The U.N. resolution on geographical names goes along the same lines.

U.N. Resolution on geographical names; III/20, 1977, names of features beyond a single sovereignty: the Conference for Geographical Standard Names, considering the need for international standardization of names of geographical features that are divided among two or more countries, makes two main recommendations.

Firstly, it recommends that countries sharing a given geographical feature under different names should endeavor, as far as possible, to reach agreement on fixing a single name for the feature concerned;

Secondly, further, it recommends that when countries sharing a given geographical feature do not succeed in agreeing on a common name, it should be a general rule of international cartography that the name used by each of the countries concerned will be accepted.

A policy of accepting only one or some of such names while excluding the rest would be inconsistent in principle as well as inexpedient in practice. Only technical reasons may sometimes make it necessary, especially in the case of small-scale maps, to dispense with the use of certain names belonging to one language or another.

In principle, nothing is definitive. A sea name can be changed by a common decision between the countries implied. A name is never given by the force of law. A geographical name is acquired by empirical practices and by the frequency and the expanse of its use. They can also come from an image, an icon, a symbol or a representation charged of sentiment and emotion of the people concerned.

The sea located between Korea, Far East Russia and Japan, is not an exception.

On April 8, 2008, Google adopted Primary Local Usage Policy for the name of the sea between Korea and Japan. Google's policy is to conform to the U.N. resolution. Google justified its policy in these terms: "As the publishers of a geographic reference tool, we believe that Google should not choose sides in international geographical disputes. For this reason, we've chosen to implement a uniform policy of Primary Local Usage. This policy is based on the principle of usage of 'primary, common, local' usage of geographical names. [...] This policy consists in writing on those maps the various names used by different countries, ethnic groups, or in different languages, to refer to the name, common places.

The adopted names are transcribed or translated into equivalent terms in different languages, varying with each linguistic version of Google Earth. As a result, East Sea / Sea of Japan in original English version is translated into 'Mer de l'Est / Mer du Japon' in French.

The same type of inscription East Sea / Sea of Japan, is applied on the internet map service of Bing / National Geographic since the spring of 2010.

Google's Primary Local Usage Policy, as like as Bing / National Geographic's practice, should be a model that the other cartographers have to follow, waiting for the adoption of a name acceptable to all parties concerned.

Li Jin-mieung

Li Jin-mieung was a junior lecturer (1983-1988), assistant professor (1988-2001) and has been professor (since 2001) at Lyon III University in France. He is also director of doctoral program for Korean studies (Doctoral School 131) at Paris VII University in France. An author of books and articles in French on modern and contemporary history of Korea, he recently published a book on Dokdo, a set of islets that make up Korea's easternmost territories, titled "Dokdo: A Korean Island Rediscovered."

Change of Meaning in "East Sea" and "Sea of Japan": Theories Shed Light on Meaning of Geographic Names [1]

Rainer Dormels

Ⅰ. Semantic Change and Geographical Names

Every word has a variety of meanings which can be added, removed, or altered over time.

Every single one of those three types of changes is a semantic change. Also geographic names can change its meaning. In this case we can theoretically differ between two types:

1. The geographic unity to which the geographic name refers to is changing.

2. The geographic name itself goes through a semantic change in the course of time.

---

1) This paper has been presented at *The 15th International Seminar on Sea Names* (2009).

Both of these kinds of semantic changes with geographic names can proceed, admittedly, also parallel and dependent of each other.

In connection with the discussion around the international naming of the sea between Korea and Japan, above all, the names 'East Sea', a literal translation of 'Donghae', or 'Sea of Japan' became used from both sides. Both names were attacked in each case by advocates of other names. Thus writes the pro-Japan homepage 'The Sea of Japan and Koreans': "There was no practice to name a body of water in large scale in East Asia. So every sea was called nebulously a name after its direction ... It is dubious that they were considered geographic names. They were common nouns rather than geographic names".

On the other hand, from the Korean side the name 'Sea of Japan' is brought into connection with the Japanese colonialism. However, the grounds given by the Korean side for it are not always understood by neutral observers. Mark Monmonier, geography professor at the Syracuse University, in his book "From Squaw Tit to Whorehouse Meadow. How Maps Name, Claim, and Inflame" (2006) for example, absolutely expresses understanding for the fact that the Koreans try to eradicate remaining traces of Japanese colonial occupation: "If I were Korean, I'd be resentful too."

However, Monmonier received a letter of a Japanese consul with a pamphlet with historical maps from a time far before the colonialism of Japan which shows the sea between Korea and Japan as 'Sea of Japan'. Monmonier was impressed: "These and other precedents support the consul's argument that the name [Sea of Japan] is unrelated to Japan's militarist or colonial past."

Reasons for misunderstandings often originated from the fact that the terms 'Donghae' and 'Sea of Japan' had different meanings in the course of time. Without considering the semantic changes an understanding of the problems of the naming of the sea between Korea and Japan is not possible.

II. Semantic Change in One of the Meanings of the Terms 'Donghae' in Korea

The term 'Donghae' has a long tradition in Korea, however, it was not always used with the same meaning. We can notice three steps of a semantic change which are not strictly separable of each other regarding to the time, but nevertheless can overlap.

These three steps are chosen in a way that the term 'Donghae', after crossing to another step, will differentiate itself in another way from other surrounding seas. Concretely: Because since a long time the sea to the east of Korea is called 'Donghae', I have chosen as a criterion for the demarcation of the three steps the names of the sea areas which lie to the west and to the south of Korea.

1. Step: 'Donghae' as the Eastern Sea in view of the sino-centric theory of the Four Seas which surround the 'continent of the middle' (China). The peninsula Korea was part of this continent. Here 'Donghae' stands in contrast to three other seas which surround the central continent. (Therefore in the strict sense, the sea area to

the west and to the south of the Korean peninsula is also a part of 'Donghae').

In China, Korea and Japan, seas in ancient times did not have proper names. One just used the terms 'Sea (海)' or 'Great Sea (大海)'. Great influence on the naming of the seas had the theory of 'Four seas'. It displays China as the empire in the middle of the world which is surrounded by four seas. This theory displays the seas after their directions as an East Sea (東海), South Sea (南海), West Sea (西海) and North Sea (北海). This Chinese world view is found in hand drawings till the 17th century. Real and idealistic views interlock here. China lies in the centre of an almost square continent. An example is the map Sihai Huayi Zongtu ("General map of China and the barbarians of the four seas") from 1532.

<Figure 1> Sihai Huayi Zongtu (1532)

In the east of the central continent one can find the peninsula Korea (朝鮮). Japan (日本) is shown as an island within the 'East Sea'. The term of ' 'Four Seas' became therefore a synonym for the (civilized) world. Thus the remark of Confucius' disciple Zi Xia 'within the four seas all people are brothers' is cited with pleasure in many official ceremonies and laudations all over the world.

There is evidence that in the beginning Koreans understood 'Donghae' in the same way as the Chinese. Therefore this means that all surrounding seas of Korea are part of 'Donghae'. On the Gwanggaeto stele (414) the name 'Donghae' is mentioned. At another place on this stele it is reported about King Yeongnak the Great, that the fame of his warlike heroic deeds were known up to the borders of the 'Four Seas'. This means that probably in this case 'Donghae' must be seen as part of the theory of 'Four Seas' and therefore it means nothing else than the waters in the east of the central continent.

2. Step: 'Donghae' as the sea to the east of the Korean peninsula as a contrast to the other two seas which surround Korea: The 'Seohae' (West Sea) to the west of the Korean peninsula and the 'Namhae' (South Sea) to the south of the Korean peninsula.

Step 2 is actually an adaptation of Step 1, but it is a smaller scale limited to Korea. This way of designating seas has also been adopted by Japan. There are some Korean maps in the 18th century which designate the waters surrounding Korea as 'Donghae (East Sea)', 'Namhae (South Sea)' and 'Seohae (West Sea)'. Also North Korea names this seas in the same way as 'East Sea of Korea' 'South Sea of Korea' and 'West Sea of Korea'.

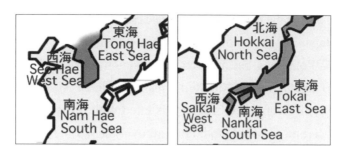

From: Watanabe/Yaji/Takizawa (2008) [2]

3. Step: 'Donghae' as a proper name for the central sea between Korea and Japan in contrast to other names for seas worldwide.

If one was still able to argue with the steps 1 and 2, that the name 'Donghae' is no 'proper' sea name, this does not apply for the third step anymore. Here the name 'Donghae' emancipates itself and differentiates itself from the 'Hwanghae' (Yellow Sea) (sea No. 51) to the west of the Korean peninsula as well as from the 'Dong-jungguk-hae' (Eastern China Sea) (sea No. 50). 'Donghae' is used in Korea instead of the worldwide used term 'Sea of Japan' and nowadays means in fact the sea No. 52 in the 3rd Edition of 'Limits of Seas and Oceans' of the IHO which also encloses parts of the 'South Sea' of Korea from step 2

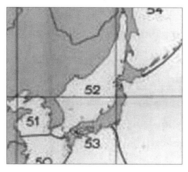

<Figure 2> *Limits of Oceans and Seas*, 3rd Edition (1953) (part)

---

2) The naming of high seas as a process of early globalization. Powerpoint - Presentation IGC Tunis 2008.

at least mainly.

'Donghae' (and respectively 'East Sea') no longer means 'the sea to the East of Korea' but 'the sea in the East of the Eurasian continent'. Schematically, the change in meaning of 'Donghae' can be classified in three steps as follows:

In Korea.net (the official website of the Republic of Korea)

Table: Change in meaning of 'Donghae' (East Sea)

	Location	Meaning
Step 1	Sea to the East of China	Sea to the East of China
Step 2	Sea to the East of Korea	Sea to the East of Korea
Step 3	Sea No. 52 in the third edition of 'Limits of Seas and Oceans'	Sea to the East of the Eurasian continent

you find the following statement: "The sea is located to the east of the Eurasian continent; and so it has been called 'East Sea' and 'Oriental Sea' for 2000 years".

But you can still find maps in Korea as a map published by the Korean Educational Development Institute in 2002 that call the sea east of Korea 'East Sea (Sea of Japan)', the sea west of Korea 'Yellow Sea' and the sea south of Korea 'South Sea'. This is a way of naming which still follows step 2 ('South Sea') mixed up with elements of step 3 ('Yellow Sea'). This careless way of mapping causes confusion, so that it would be helpful to avoid the name 'South Sea' in this kind of maps published by official Korean organizations and institutions.

In summary one can say that the term 'Donghae' has a long tradition in Korea, its meaning, admittedly, as it is the case with many terms, has changed in the course of time. This semantic change includes also, but not only changes of the geographic unity which is called 'Donghae'. If 'Donghae' was still a part of a sino-centric world view in the first step, it developed in the second step to a term which designates one of the seas surrounding the respective country like Korea of Japan. Then in the third step the term 'Donghae' becomes a modern sea name which, while one took over the name 'Yellow Sea' for the 'West Sea' in Korea, the name of the sea area to the east of Korea was deliberately maintained as 'East Sea', although Japanese and other maps preferred the name 'Sea of Japan'.

Ⅲ. The Semantic Change of the Name 'Sea of Japan' through Japanese Colonialism

Toponyms which are insulting are subject to substitute. Monmonier mentions in his earlier cited book among others following examples:

old: Chinaman Spring - new: Chinese Spring

old: Polack lake - new: Corner lake

In 1963 all entries on maps that includes the word 'Nigger' were substituted by 'Negro' through the U.S. Board on Geographic Names, in 1974 'Jap' became in a similar manner 'Japanese'. At that time 'Negro' was still seen as polite wording, later on it became negative too. While one sees the problematic of using toponyms like Chinaman Spring, Polack Lake, Niggerhead Point or Squaw Tit Peak at first sight, someone is only able to recognize a countries problem with a certain name if he knows the historical and geographical circumstances.

As an example from the German-speaking we can talk about the abbreviation 'Tschechei' for Czech Republic. The official German name is 'Tschechische Republik (Czech Republic)'. There are two unofficial abbreviations 'Tschechien' and 'Tschechei' in German. However, there were protests against the term 'Tschechei' in the Czech Republic, although it is also used by many Czechs if they speak German. The name 'Tschechei' is associated with the Nazi time (1933-1945). However, fact is that in general the term 'Tschechei' has nothing to do with Nazis. The name appears latest since 1918, so clearly before the Nazis take-over of power.

However, if one still assumes a connection with the Nazi time, then because the Nazis have used the term 'Rest-Tschechei' in their propaganda. The aim of the Nazi dictatorship was the suppression of Czechoslovakia (1938/39). The formerly neutral term 'Tschechei' got therefore a negative meaning. Now in addition to its old neutral meaning the name 'Tschechei' had also got a second negative meaning: Many German-speaking people did not stop to use the name 'Tschechei' in its neutral meaning. However the Czech Republic has protested against the use of the name 'Tschechei', and this has led to the fact that many have followed the wish of the neighboring state, so that the name 'Tschechei' has disappeared from the German-speaking newspapers and is not used anymore. Instead most people use the term 'Tschechien' and who does not like it or has the feeling that he was forced to use this name says just 'Tschechische Republik'.

What does however mean 'Sea of Japan'? When Europeans gave the name to this sea the name 'Sea of Japan' had the neutral meaning of a sea which lies beside Japan.

At the 10th International Seminar on the Naming of Seas in Paris in 2004 Kim Shin states in the first edition of 'Limits of Oceans and Seas' of the IHO (1928) among 26 seas the 'Sea of Japan' was the only one that was named after one single state: "According to the 'Limits of Oceans and Seas' it what indicated that in giving the name to a sea lying between two states, they follow the principle of giving the name of a specific country. Instead it is preferred to use a name related to a continent, or to use a third name. Alternatively, both names may be recorded together."

Kim speaks here of a 'sea lying between two states', however, the problem is that the Japanese and everybody those who have not recognized Korea as an independent state have seen this agenda completely different. The 'Sea of Japan' was not seen as a sea between two states, but as a sea between two parts of Japan, as a sea which lies between the Japanese islands and the Japanese province Chosen (Korea).

As a result of the Japanese colonialism and expansionism the name 'Sea of Japan' underwent a semantic change. After 1910 the 'Sea of Japan' not only had the meaning 'sea which borders Japan'. Now the name 'Sea of Japan' also meant "sea between two parts of Japan, the inland sea of Japan." In this second meaning the use of the name 'Sea of Japan' means in fact that the peninsula to the west of the 'Sea of Japan', namely Korea, is part of Japan.

By the fact that Japan has transformed the Korean East Sea into an inland sea of Japan the name 'Sea of Japan' became a symbol for Japanese imperialism and is therefore intolerable for Koreans.

So, in the case of the name 'Sea of Japan' it is important that this term has received a new meaning because of the colonization of Korea by Japan in addition, namely an inland sea of Japan.

Schematically, the change in meaning of 'Sea of Japan' can be classified in two steps as follows:

Table: Change of meaning of 'Sea of Japan'

	Meaning
Step 1	Sea to the West of Japan
Step 2 (from 1910 on)	Meaning 1: Sea to the West of Japan Meaning 2: inland sea within the colonialist Japan

Therefore, if Korea begins to approach against the sole use of the name 'Sea of Japan', the reason should not be resentful feelings for Japan. It should not be a matter of wanting to show up Japan on account of its past. Not the fact that the name 'Japan' is part of a sea name is the problem. Korea and Japan have stepped up more and more to each other the last years. Japanese youngsters see Korean TV series, Korean youngsters hear J-pop.

However, as a result of progressing globalization and worldwide sensitivity on inappropriate and discriminating names the wish of the Korean people to prevent the sole use of the name 'Sea of Japan' becomes bigger and bigger. Just as the use of the word 'Tschechei' reminds Czechs of the use of this word by the Nazis, the same happens to Koreans with the use of the word 'Sea of Japan' as it reminds them involuntarily of the 'Japanese Inland Sea', wittingly or unwittingly. If one considers the semantic change of the name 'Sea of Japan', don't we have to understand, why Koreans associate this name directly with colonialism?

IV. Increased Sensitivity on Terms – a Global Trend

Not only have the meanings of the geographic terms changed in course of the time, also the sensitivity of the people towards them. The name 'East Sea(Donghae)' has a long tradition in Korea and is a part of a cultural heritage which shows specific Korean features, but also crosses national borders.

Therefore, the conflict between Korea and Japan concerning an adequate naming of the sea between both nations is so difficult to solve, because one can not expect on the one hand that the Koreans further accept the term 'Sea of Japan' as the only valid one, nevertheless, on the other hand, it is unrealistic to expect that Japan will support a change of the existing name actively. Finally, in case of the sea between Korea and Japan, the ones who are responsible for the naming of the seas worldwide are required to find a suitable compromise which takes into consideration the feelings of both nations.

Rainer Dormels

Rainer Dormels is a professor for Korean Studies at the University of Vienna. Dormels graduated with a Masters of Arts degree in Korean linguistics from Seoul National University and earned his doctoral degree in Korean Studies at the University of Hamburg. Dormels' research has also received support from the Northeast Asian History Foundation and Seoul National University.

Usage of "East Sea" in Scientific, and Reference Literature [1]

Norman Cherkis

I. Background

Maritime toponyms refer to large and small bodies of water and to undersea features. Surface regions i.e., 'seas' and 'oceans', have been delineated and boundaries have been published in the International Hydrographic Bureau publication, S-23, of which the last edition was published in 1953. Some of the names have been used for hundreds and sometimes thousands of years as in the case of the 'East Sea'. The present-day international maritime community, including most governmental agencies however, has been using the term, 'Sea of Japan', exclusively for that body of water for most of the last 100 years or so. A new edition of publication S-23 has been planned for the past 20 years, but because of disagreements between certain members of the IHO, no final text has been distributed, and until the disagreeing parties resolve their differences, the publication of a revised S-23 is

---

1) This paper has been presented at *The 14th International Seminar on Sea Names - Geography, Sea Names, and Undersea Feature Names* (2008).

impossible.

The reason for using the Sea of Japan term is mainly because Imperial Japan aggressively annexed Korea in the early 20th century, and for the next 40 years, Japan embarked on a campaign to systematically remove all vestiges of Korean heritage, including the Korean language.

This practice continued until the end of the World War II in 1945. After cessation of hostilities, the Korean nation was reestablished in the company of nations of the world and the Korean language was likewise resurrected. Underscoring the importance of the sea's name is the new South Korean national anthem which has, as its first two words, 'Dong Hae …' which translates to 'East Sea' in English.

The use of the toponym, 'East Sea' or, in Korean, 'Dong Hae' can be traced back at least two millennia. At that time, ancient China dominated the region and used the term 'East Sea' to indicate that direction from their eastern coastline. The Chinese documents that eluded destruction during informational 'purges' of several Chinese emperors over the past 2,000 years are now housed in great historical libraries mostly located in China and Korea. In South Korea, a reference to 'Dong Hae' appears on a stele to King Gwanggaeto and dates to the year 414 of the Common Era.

The name 'East Sea' was established for at least 1,000 years before Japan was even known to exist to the Western World. The first Western reference to the 'East Sea' is attributed to a world map created in the 13th century, outlining the travels of Giovanni

<Figure 1> Portion of the copy of the di Plano Carpini map of 1434. Maereum Orientale (East Sea) is clearly visible near the upper right portion of the land masses.

di Plano Carpini in eastern and Central Asia between 1245-1247, C.E. That map is unfortunately lost, but a copy from ca.1434 is known to exist, and it presently resides at Yale University.

The first written reference to the 'Sea of Japan' known to exist in Western writings is that of the Roman Catholic missionary-priest, Matteo Ricci. S.J., the founder of Catholic Missions in China after 1582 C.E, some 148 years after the copied di Plano Carpini map was published. It is possible, even probable that Father Ricci used the Carpini map, but used the name 'Sea of Japan' in a 1602 document in which a map was included. A number of scholarly papers and monographs have been published regarding usage of the 'East Sea' and the 'Sea of Japan', including variations thereof and arguments for which name should be used in the 21st century, but these do need to be mentioned here. These arguments can be found in great detail by searching on the terms 'East Sea' and

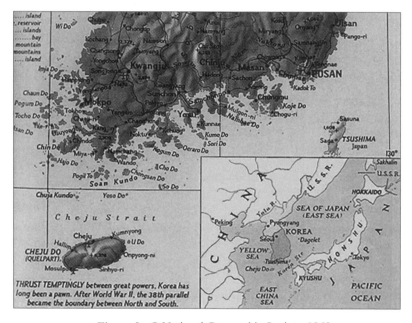

<Figure 2> © National Geographic Society, 1969

'Sea of Japan' on Internet search engines. The arguments, most of which are nationalistic in nature were written mainly by South Korean and Japanese authors who wish to establish a proper toponym for the body of water between Korea and Japan. Some of these arguments have been particularly unflattering to the side with the opposing opinions, resulting in emotional interchanges, again, posted mostly on Internet blogs.

Moving toward the 21st century we must pause, because in March 1969, the National Geographic Society – an international geography and map publisher of great regard throughout the world – published a map of Korea on page 308 of an article that shows the name, East Sea used as an alternate name for the 'Sea of Japan'.

Presently, all major producers of family, school and scholarly atlases, e.g., the Times Atlas, Rand-McNally World Atlas, Langenscheidt Publishers Atlas, Collins World Atlas, National Geographic World Atlas, et al., all give equal importance to the body of water called the 'East Sea' and/or the 'Sea of Japan'.

II. 'East Sea' / 'Sea of Japan' Toponyms

'East Sea'/'Sea of Japan' toponyms discussed here deal mainly with features completely outside of the territorial limits of the nations that border the region, i.e., beyond 12 nautical miles from the shores of Korea, Japan and Russia.

Early 20th century maps note the existence of the Korea/Tsushima Strait, that body of water that separates Korea and Japan and though which a branch of the oceanographically important Kuroshio Current flows northward. The Strait contains a historically Japanese island, Tsushima, hence it was given the name, Tsushima Strait a bit over 100 years ago, during the beginning of the colonial annexation period. However, a significant number of Western publications, dating from the middle 1850s, show it as Korea

Strait, or the equivalent in other Indo European tongues, e.g., as 'detroit de Corée' in French. Some of these maps also refer to the East Sea as 'La Mer du Corée', or 'Sea of Korea'. No organization dedicated standardization of maritime geographic terminology body, e.g., the IHB, existed at the time.

Tsushima Basin is a name applied to a more-or less-circular depression in the southwestern-most 'East Sea'/'Sea of Japan'. According to IHO/IOC publication B-6 guidelines, "The first choice of a specific term, where feasible, should be one associated with a geographical feature: e.g., Aleutian Ridge, Aleutian Trench ..." The nearest geographical feature to this depression is Ulleung-do (Ulleung Island), and therefore, according to the IHO/IOC principles for naming undersea features, should be called Ulleung Basin because the basin is immediately adjacent to Ulleung-do.

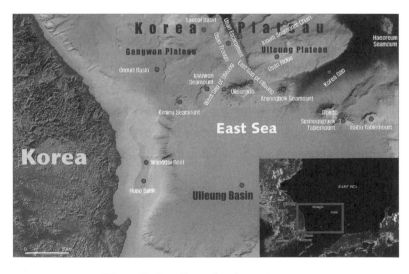

<Figure 3> Locations of undersea toponyms.
(Ocean Atlas of Korea 'East Sea'; NORI, Republic of Korea, 2007)

However, since the name Tsushima Basin has been previously used in the scientific and geographic literature, and almost exclusively between 1910 and 1970 due to political events that will not again revisited. Tsushima Basin should be retained as a variant name within gazetteers, or used concurrently with Ulleung Basin, as can be seen in the appended reference list.

During the 20th meeting of the GEBCO Sub-Committee on Undersea Feature Names (GEBCO-SCUFN) in Monaco in June of 2007, the recently-formed Korean Committee on Undersea Feature Names (K-CUF) submitted ten names for approval by the Sub-Committee. Those names are Anyongbok Seamount, Gangwon Plateau, Hupo Bank, Igyuwon Seamount, Kimmu Seamount, Onnuri Basin, Saenal Basin, Ulleung Plateau, Usan Escarpment and Usan Trough. Most of these features were recently discovered in the East Sea/Sea of Japan by Korean research ships. (fig. 3). All of these features were approved by unanimous vote of the GEBCO Sub-Committee and were placed in the GEBCO Gazetteer of Undersea Feature Names (IHO-IOC Publication, B-8).

At the 21st meeting of GEBCO-SCUFN in mid-May, 2008, at which time the Korean Committee on Undersea Feature Names (K-CUFN) proposed eight new undersea feature names, four of which are in the 'East Sea': Jugam Ridge, Ulsan Seachannel, Usan Ridge and Wangdol Reef. All of the names were approved by the GEBCO-SCUFN committee and added to the GEBCO gazetteer.

Ⅲ. Statistics

In 2006, an extensive literature search of non-Korean-language publications was initiated to locate print media articles that support the Korean position that alternate names and dual usage of the term, 'East Sea' can be and have been used within the science community. At the time of this writing, 694 papers have been located in published literature and governmental sources which contain 'East Sea'/'Sea of Japan' toponyms. For relevance in this paper only, the subaerial toponyms have been limited to the following: 'East Sea'/'Sea of Japan'.

Of the 694 papers, 519 contain the toponym, 'East Sea', in either the title or in the text. Further, of the entire list of 580 references, 309 contain the names of non-Korean authors, many of whom are from Japan.

Norman Cherkis

Norman Cherkis is an active member of the Advisory Committee on Undersea Features of the US Board on Geographic Names and a long-standing member of the Subcommittee on Undersea Feature Names of the General Bathymetric Chart of the Oceans, both of which deal with seafloor toponyms.

He has more than 45 years of experience in the field of marine geo-sciences, and for the past 11 years, he has operated his own business, Five Oceans Consultant, Ltd., providing consulting services and expertise to public-, private-, non-profit- and academic organizations around the world.

"Donghae" and "Nihonkai" – "East Sea" and "Sea of Japan": Are They Exonyms or Allonyms, and Is There a Missing Term? [1]

Naftali Kadmon

Can different parts of a maritime geographical feature carry names of different terminological status? The following remarks attempt to supply an answer to this question, in particular with reference to the two maritime toponyms in the heading.

Ⅰ. History

The sea between the Japanese archipelago and the Peninsula of Korea is, today, named in most western maps and atlases 'Sea of Japan', a translation of the Japanese name Nihon Kai. Some fifteen years ago the Republic of Korea, at the Sixth United Nations Conference on the Standardization of Geographical Names, requested that the toponymy of this sea be changed officially,

1) This paper has been presented at *The 13ᵗʰ International Seminar on the Naming and East Sea* (2007).

so that the Korean name, Donghae, that is, 'East Sea', could be embodied in it. The reasons cited by the Republic of Korea were, among others, that the prevalent name points to a sort of possession, and since this sea does not 'belong' to the country of the rising sun, a Korean name should also be given to it. Japan resisted this proposal, and has been doing so ever since. The Sixth and the Seventh United Nations Conferences asked the two sides to consult together in order to find a solution acceptable to both – as yet without results.

The sea concerned, and certainly its central and major part, lies outside the territorial waters of any one country. The Republic of Korea has organized thirteen international seminars, chiefly devoted to the naming of seas and in particular to the name Donghae, 'East Sea'. These seminars were attended by experts from different countries, among them representatives from Japan which, however, did not represent any governmental or other executive authority. At first, in order to replace the name 'Sea of Japan' by a single unbiased or non-aligned name acceptable to both sides, several neutral names were proposed such as Blue Sea, Sea of Peace, etc. This would have been in line with the principle of 'one place – one name' applied for example by the United States Board on Geographic Names to its domestic toponymy. For a discussion of this principle see for example Kadmon (2001)[2] and UNGEGN (United Nations Group of Experts on Geographical Names) (2006)[3].

---

2) Kadmon, Naftali (2001), Why Standardization? Who Benefits from It?, *Toponymy: The Lore, Laws and Language of Geographical Names*, New York : Vantage Press. pp. 187-189.
3) United Nations Group of Experts on Geographical Names (2006), *Manual for the Na-*

Later, when none of these names was accepted by Japan, Korea's drive was directed towards a bilingual solution – namely, having this sea carry two names side-by-side, one Japanese and one Korean (or *vice versa*). There are, of course, many maritime areas around the world carrying two or more allonyms without any of the sides objecting to the other's name. While Japan claimed that the name 'Sea of Japan' is the preferred name worldwide, the Republic of Korea stated – and graphically demonstrated in a number of special publications that the name Sea of Korea or 'East Sea' enjoyed great antiquity. Japan later countered with similar graphic examples showing the wide distribution of the name 'Sea of Japan' especially in the last two centuries. As mentioned above, with Japan demanding the exclusive application of its preferred name because any other solution would lead to confusion and disorientation, no solution to the problem has as yet been found. The Republic of Korea then turned to cartographic institutions worldwide, and this resulted in bilingual cases where the name 'East Sea' appears in maps alongside the name 'Sea of Japan'. Korea strives to increase the number of these cases.

Ⅱ. Terminology and Cartography

The question now arises: what is – or would be – the terminological status of the two toponyms under consideration? Do they conform

---

tional Standardization of Geographical Names, New York : United Nations. pp. 36, 83.

to the definitions in the *Glossary of Terms for the Standardization of Geographical Names*[4]? Following are the reflections of the undersigned (who serves as editor of the six-language United Nations *Glossary*), from a purely toponymic-terminological and cartographic viewpoint.

(i) According to the Law of the Sea (1982, 1994) "…jurisdiction refers to the power of a state to affect persons, property and **circumstances** within its territory," which includes its maritime zones. Over those parts of the sea which come under the definition of territorial waters, the respective states have authority of conferring maritime names – which comes under the term 'circumstances' mentioned above. These names are then endonyms – and if ratified by a national authority, even official endonyms.

(ii) Areas lying outside territorial waters (and not covered by any national jurisdiction) can carry any name applied to them by different linguistic or political communities such as different countries. By 'carrying' a name is meant its being used on the one hand in written verbal documents, such as in literature and particularly in geographical gazetteers and indexes, and on the other hand in graphics such as maps and maritime charts. None of these names can be regarded as an endonym, an endonym being defined by the *Glossary of Terms for the Standardization of Geographical Names* (term No. 076) as "name of a geographical feature in one of the

---

4) United Nations Group of Experts on Geographical Names (2002), *Glossary of Terms for the Standardization of Geographical Names*, New York : United Nations.

languages occurring in that area where the feature is situated." No language can be said to 'occur' in the high seas. However, after defining what they are not (that is, endonyms), the different names applied by different countries are allonyms (term No. 005): alternative (and taxonomically undefined) names for a single geographical entity.

(iii) Any country can apply its own preferred names even on geographical items (in the present case – maritime features) which are covered by the jurisdiction of another country, for example, in that country's territorial waters. Such a name will then be defined as an exonym. In the *Glossary of Terms for the Standardization of Geographical Names* this was defined by term No. 081. In a joint session of the UNGEGN Working Groups on Terminology and Exonyms in 2006, it was decided to amend the definition as follows (and this was ratified by the 9th United Nations Conference on the Standardization of Geographical Names): name used in a specific language for a geographical feature situated outside the area where that language is spoken, and differing in its form from the name used in an official or well-established language of the area where the geographical feature is situated. Examples: Mailand is the German exonym for Milano (Italian); *Jerusalen* is the Spanish exonym for *Yerushalayim* (Hebrew); *Lake Constance* is the English exonym for *Bodensee* (German). Thus, *Donghae* (East Sea) would be a Korean exonym for the Japanese territorial waters part of the sea under consideration, as would be the Japanese name '*Sea of Japan*' covering Korean territorial waters.

Ⅲ. Definitions

The two names which are the subject of the present paper can thus be classified and defined as follows.

1.1 The name Nihon Kai or 'Sea of Japan' is an (official?) maritime endonym within those waters that are regarded by the international community as coming under Japan's jurisdiction.

1.2 The terminological status of the toponym 'Sea of Japan' as applied to the international parts of this body of water (the 'high sea') is still undefined (see below). But no objection on formal grounds can be validly raised against this name.

1.3 The use of the name 'Sea of Japan' in respect of the territorial waters of the Republic of Korea generates a Japanese exonym.

Now, to the opposite, western side of this sea:

2.1 The name Donghae or 'East Sea' is an (official?) maritime endonym in respect of the territorial waters of the Republic of Korea.

2.2 The terminological status of the toponym 'East Sea' as applied to the international parts of this sea (the 'high sea'), is still undefined. But here, too, no valid objection on formal grounds can be raised against the use of this name.

2.3 The use of the name 'East Sea' if referring to the territorial waters of Japan constitutes a Korean exonym.

It should be pointed out that it is common practice, by any particular country or map producer, to cover in its small-scale maps the territorial waters of any other country or countries under its general allonym for the sea of which these territorial waters are a part, and thus in theory generating exonyms. One example out of many would be the Swedish name *Östersjön* for the different names of the Baltic Sea applied by the countries bordering it, whose territorial-waters endonyms then become Swedish exonyms.

Summing up,

(a) Concerning the international waters or 'high sea', both names 'Sea of Japan' and 'East Sea' are neither endonyms nor exonyms. They are allonyms undefined from a terminological point of view, and they have equal status.

(b) The names 'Sea of Japan' and 'East Sea', if applied to or covering the territorial waters of the opposite side, constitute exonyms. This can also be expressed in a different form: if and where these names cover (for example in charts and maps) the entire sea, they constitute exonyms where they cover territorial waters of the opposing side. However, in maps of small scale, they will usually not be separately indicated.

In conclusion, any country and any cartographic institution can employ either, and preferably both names, to the 'high' or international areas of the sea under discussion.

Finally, from the above discussion it follows that there is a need for a new term to be added to the *Glossary of Terms for the Standardization of Geographical Names*, namely the status of a toponym for a maritime feature in international waters. It also seems that the term univocity used in the UNGEGN Manual (see above) for the 'one place – one name' principle is a misnomer, univocity (from Latin vox, voice) meaning 'having only one meaning'[5], and not 'only one name'. Suitable proposals for amendments to the *Glossary of Terms* were presented to UNGEGN's Working Group on Toponymic Terminology but have not yet been acted upon.

---

5) See, for example, *Webster's New International Dictionary*, 'univocal' and 'univocity'.

Naftali Kadmon

Emeritus Professor Naftali Kadmon, B.A., M.Sc., Ph.D., has been lecturing on cartography and toponymy at the Hebrew University of Jerusalem for 25 years. Since 1977 and until retiring in 2007 he represented his country at United Nations institutions on geographical names, among others as chairman of UNGEGN's working group on terminology and as editor of the U.N. six-language *Glossary of Terms for the Standardization of Geographical Names*. An author of several books on toponymy in Hebrew, English and Japanese, he still serves as chairman of the Israeli Government Names Commission's Committee on Geographical Names.

A Historical Focus

Understanding of the "East Sea" in Korean History

Lee Sangtae

References to the "East Sea" in Ancient Chinese
Literature

Han Maoli

Russian Geographical Investigations of North-Eastern
Asia Seas in ⅩⅦ – ⅩⅧ Centuries

Sergey Ganzey

Understanding of the 'East Sea' in Korean History

Lee Sangtae

I. Introduction

Since the Korean Peninsula is surrounded by water on three sides, Korea has had a keen interest in its waters throughout history. The sea area between the Korean Peninsula and the Japanese Archipelago has been called the 'East Sea' in Korea based on the Oriental Thoughts of the Five Elements. More specifically, the names of sea areas surrounding the Korean Peninsula were created based on the combination of the four cardinal directions – north, south, east, wes – and the space concept of the 'Five Elements'. The 'East Sea' was the one which was located to the east of the Peninsula.

The first record of the name 'East Sea' can be traced back to a description by King Dongmyeong of the Goguryeo Kingdom in 'The History of the Three Kingdoms' in B.C. 59. Meanwhile, the country name 'Japan' first appeared in 670 around 700 years after Korea began using the name 'East Sea' and the appellation Sea of Japan first appeared in 1602 in a map dubbed 'Mappamondo

(Complete Map of the World)' by Matteo Ricci, an Italian Catholic missionary based in Beijing. Therefore, the name 'Sea of Japan' was first used about 1,650 years after the Koreans began calling the sea area, 'East Sea'.

II. Understanding of the 'East Sea' during the Three Kingdom Era

The reference to 'East Sea' was found in *Samguksagi* and *Samgukyoosa* which are the history books of the Three Kingdoms. According to the history records, 'East Sea' had great significance to the people of the Three Kingdoms in national security, and natural disasters.

1. National Security – Protection of the Fatherland

The 'East Sea' became the focus of attention of the Shilla dynasty (one of the Three Kingdoms) mainly because of frequent aggressions of Japanese raiders across the 'East Sea'. Since B.C. 50 (the 8th year of King Parkhyukguse), foreign powers invaded the Shilla territory. In A.D. 14 (the 11th year of King Chachawoon), about 100 Japanese warships raided and looted the villages located along the 'East Sea', and the King of Shilla dispatched the central forces to hold off the attack. Shilla established a friendly relationship with the Japanese to avoid invasions in A.D. 59 (the 3rd year of King Talhae). However, the Japanese raiders attacked the country in A.D. 73(the 17th year of King Talhae) only about

10 years later. The frequent invasions of the Japanese raiders were a major cause of worry.

It was King Munmu who responded strongly against such invasions. Since he achieved the unification of the Three Kingdoms, there was little worry over any invasion of Japanese by land. However, he was very concerned about a possible invasion of Japanese raiders across the East Sea. He vowed that after his death he would become a water dragon so that he could continue to protect the country. He had his ashes placed in a rock pile in the ocean. Obeying his will, the remains of King Munmu's cremated body were buried under a rock in the 'East Sea'. The rock is now called 'Daewangam Rock'. Sinmu who succeeded King Munmu built the Gameunsa (Temple) to obey King Munmu's wishes to defend the fatherland. A record on A Korean traditional bamboo flute called 'Man-pa-sik-jeok'. In a recording using a bamboo flute, 'Man-Pa-Sik-Jeok', indicates his love for the United Shilla Kingdom as follows;

"In the 3rd year of King Sinmu's reign, he ordered a bamboo tree cut on a small island in the East Sea and makes a bamboo flute."

Later, Kings Hyoseong (742) and Seondeok (785) were cremated and their ashes were scattered into the East Sea according to their last wishes. This demonstrates that the kings of Shilla wished to protect and defend their country even after death.

2. Natural Disasters and the 'East Sea'

During the era of the Three Kingdoms when science and techno-logy were much less developed compared with the present, the people deeply felt concern and fear over natural phenomena.

They thought sudden natural phenomena were revelations of the god to the king. For example, three big fish about 30 and 12 feet in length and height appeared in the 'East Sea' in 256 (the 15th year of King Jeom-hae's reign). And a big fish with a horn was caught in the 'East Sea' in 416 (the 15th year of King Sil-seong's reign), and it was as big as a wagon. Probably the big fish might be whales.

When the East Sea turned red and its temperature rose in 639 (the 8th year of Queen Seondeok's reign), many dead fish floated to the surface of the water. In 699 (the 8th year of King Hyoso's reign), the 'East Sea' again turned red. In September during King Dong's reign, the water of the 'East Sea' violently collapsed onto each other like waves in a battle, and the sound was heard as far as Gyeongju. Drums and small gongs sometimes began ringing on their own. In 915 (the 4th year of King Sindeok's reign), the waters of the Champo Sea Heunghae-eup Yeongil-gun in Gyeongsangbuk-do) and the water of the 'East Sea' 'fought' for three days in a row, and waves rolled up as high as 70 meters. People of Shilla were in awe of unexpected natural phenomena like these.

Ⅲ. Understanding of the East Sea during the Koryo Kingdom

As the capital was moved to Songak in the age of the Koryo Kingdom, the people of the Kingdom had more interest in the West Sea than the 'East Sea'. The salient feature of the people's perception on the 'East Sea' in this era was that the people performed sacrificial rites for the East Sea.

Sacrificial rites for the guardian spirits of mountains, rivers, and seas were prevalent in the Koryo Kingdom. There were shrines for the 'East Sea', the West Sea, and the South Sea.

According to geography books of the Koryo Kingdom, the shrine for the 'East Sea' was in Yikryeong-hyeon, Gyoju-do (currently Gangwon-do). *The Yearbook of Yangyang-Dohobu* in the Chronicles of King Sejong indicates that Yikryeong-hyeon is Yangyang city at present. *Dong-Guk-Yeo-Ji-Seung-Nam* (a geography book), *Yeo-Ji-Do-Seo*, and *Dae-Dong-Ji-Ji* which were published during the Joseon Dynasty state that the shrine for the East Sea was in Yangyang-Dohobu. Yang Seong-ji, who served as a high ranking courtier for King Sejo of the Joseon Dynasty, set forth in his proposal presented to the King, "As the shrines for the East, West, and South Seas were built centering around Gaeseong which used to be the capital of the Koryo Kingdom, they have to be moved centering the new capital 'Hanyang'." He suggested that the shrine for the 'East Sea' had to be moved to Gangneung, the one for the West Sea to Inchcon, and the one for the South Sea to Suncheon, respectively. The Yang Seong-ji's proposal to the king indicates that there were shrines for the East, West, and South Seas during the Koryo Kingdom.

Ⅳ. The Joseon Dynasty and the East Sea

During the Joseon Dynasty, the 'East Sea' was given significant attention. Whenever a severe drought hit the nation, people believed that they needed to find a 'devoted' daughter-in-law living around the coast of 'East Sea' areas to overcome the dried weather based on folk beliefs. In particular, 'East Sea' was praised as a sacred place to wash away sins or disgrace.

1. Drought and the East Sea

Since the Joseon Dynasty adopted the 'agriculture-firs' principle, it prepared several countermeasures against drought. For instance, when dry weather continued throughout the nation, the government released prisoners or sought fast progress in trials with the belief that the drought was caused because someone was falsely charged and imprisoned.

Whenever a drought would continue, the people were also reminded of an old story, 'the devoted daughter-in-law of the 'East Sea'. According to the story, after a filial daughter-in-law bearing a grudge died, drought continued in the village for three years.

This old story was quoted from King Taejong's reign to King Jeongjo's reign whenever the nation suffered a drought. The 'East Sea' in the story was actually a village name in the Han Dynasty, China, but it was quoted during the Joseon Dynasty as if it had been the 'East Sea' during this time.

2. Sacred Place of the 'East Sea' & Poems Praising the 'East Sea'

The 'East Sea' was praised as a sacred place during the Joseon dynasty, which was the biggest difference from before. In particular, the Joseon Dynasty saw the 'East Sea' as a subject for appreciation. A song, entitled *The Song of the Heonnamsan Mountain*, written during King Sejong's reign, says, "The 'East Sea' used to be calm... politely offered the Namsansu to the King... wish that the King will be the father of the people for a long time..." Another song, entitled *The Song of Knowledge and Virtue*, praised the East Sea, "As the 'East Sea' washes off the bad hearts of people, it will live forever. Since the East Sea obeys God's will and acts in concert with the public mind, God will bless our life."

A song, entitled *The Song of the Leader*, written during King Sejo's reign, says, "This chivalrous spirit was a great help for them to obey God's will. The 'East Sea' completely cleared the dirty virtue and it will be clean forever."

Yoo Yang-chun, a high-ranking member of the Board of Punish ment during King Seongjon's reign, offered a song to the King, saying, "All people prayed to God for a blessing as much as the water of the East Sea and for longevity like Namsan Mountain. Their prayers were spread throughout the world." They wished for God's blessing like the East Sea.

King Seongjong bestowed a collection of a Buddhist cannon of Scriptures to Japan in 1488 (the 19th year of King Seongjong), and the Japanese government sent a letter of appreciation to the King of the Joseon Dynasty stating "We can never thank you enough for the gift from you. The gratitude we feel would be indescribable if we pump up water from the 'East Sea' and make all bamboos on the Namsan Mountain black. We express a sincere appreciation to you."

Furthermore, the filial piety of King Jeongjo and King Sunjo was compared to the 'East Sea'. In particular, King Sunjo's love and respect for his parents were praised as follows, "The King received two cups from the 7 stars of the Big Dipper, poured the water from the 'East Sea' into the cups, and offered them to his parents. We can never praise the King enough."

King Gojong issued a statement to congratulate his mother's 60th birthday in 1868 (the 5th year of King Gojong's reign), saying, "I offered a cup of wine to my dear mother on the first day of the year when everyone is blessed and all creation are shining. The respect and happiness I feel for my mother is as deep as the 'East Sea'. I pray to God she will live as long as Namsan Mountain."

As explained above, the 'East Sea' drew praise and admiration during the Joseon dynasty and was recognized as a source of blessing. It indicates that the 'East Sea' has long been a place that deeply moved and inspired the Korean people as shown in the lyrics of the national anthem.

Ⅴ. Conclusion

Mountains, rivers, and seas originally did not have names, but over time names were given to them with the development of human culture. Since the Korean Peninsula is surrounded by water on three sides, the people have had a strong interest in its waters. They probably began using the name 'East Sea' because it was the water located in the east. The first record of the name 'East Sea' can be traced back to a description of King Dongmyeong of the Goguryeo Kingdom. It was before the Three Kingdoms were founded indicating that the name 'East Sea' has long been used by the Korean people since antiquity.

During Koryo and the early Joseon Dynasty, the people held sacrificial rites for the 'East Sea', and in particular, the people of Joseon thought of the 'East Sea' as a sacred place. Later, the 'East Sea' was even mentioned in the first line of the Korean national anthem, "Until the 'East Sea' and the Backdusan (mountain) are worn away......" Like this, the appellation 'East Sea' has a long history that goes back two thousand years, and about 75million Koreans still call the sea area the 'East Sea'.

Lee Sangtae

Lee Sangtae is a professor of the Korea International Culture University of Graduate. He also serves as director of the Historical Materials Research Office and the History Research & Compilation Office at the National Institute of Korean History. He is currently vice president of the Society for East Sea.

References to the "East Sea" in Ancient Chinese Literature [1)]

Han Maoli

The sea area to the east of the Korean Peninsula, which is located west of the Japanese archipelago and southwest of Sakhalin (Ku Ye Island), is called either the 'East Sea' or 'Sea of Japan'. The documents of ancient China indicate that this sea area began to have its own name during the Tang(唐) Dynasty (618-907), nearly 1,500 years ago. At that time, the sea area was called 'Xiao Sea' (小海), 'Shao Sea' (少海) or 'Southern Sea' (南海) by Chinese people. But the meaning of the name only refers to parts of the sea area to the east of the Korean Peninsula, not the whole area. We can confirm that the documents of the Tang Dynasty did not contain the proper name referring to this whole sea area.

The name 'East Sea', recorded in the literature of the Lao(辽) and Jin(金) dynasties (906-1279), continued to be used by the local residents Nu Zhen(女真) and their Manchurian descendants. Some other names also appeared during that period, but it still cannot be used as the proper name for the whole sea area. Moreover,

---

1) This paper has been presented at *The 14th International Seminar on Sea Names - Geography, Sea Names, and Undersea Feature Names* (2008).

although the northern part of the Sea of Japan was named the 'Jing Sea' or 'Jing Chuan Sea' in the Yuan Dynasty(1279-1368) and the name 'East Sea' was not found in the literature of that time, we can assume that 'East Sea' was continually used from the Liao and Jin dynasties, because the Manchurians during the Ming and Qing dynasties, the offspring of Nu Zhen, lived along western coast of this sea area during Yuan Dynasty.

The article Ji Dong Hai Zhu Wen(祭东海祝文) printed in the book *Da Jin Ji Li*(大金集礼) provides some proof that the name 'East Sea' was applied to this sea by the Nu Zhen people, the residents living on the western coast of China nearly 1,000 years ago. After the Jin Dynasty, Manchurian, the descendant of Nu Zhen, accepted the name 'East Sea' from their ancestors. Because the relations between the northeast China and the central part were not close enough to make the name popular, we seldom see references to the 'East Sea' in the documents of that time. In the 17th century, when the Manchurians rose in the northeast to found the Qing Government, the name 'East Sea' was popular again and it reappeared in the books of that time frequently. In conclusion, 'East Sea' was the first name of this sea area. It was used from the Liao and Jin Dynasty until the late Qing Dynasty (1644-1911).

Apart from the name 'East Sea', 'Korean East Sea' was also used as the name for this sea area in the literature of the Ming Dynasty (1368-1644) as *Hai Fang Zuan Yao* (海防篡要, Introduction of Coastal Defense) and *Wan Li San Da Zheng* (万历三大征, Three Expeditions of Emperor Wan Li, 1573-1620). *Hai Fang Zuan Yao* (海防篡要, Introduction of Coast Defense), altogether 13 volumes including one volume of maps, was written by Wang Zaijin(王在晋), who was a general in charge of the coast defense from Liaoning to Shandong Province. He was very familiar with the sea areas around northern China. The book, based on his knowledge and other works about coastal defense, describes the details of the sea areas around China and Korea, and the key aspects of coastal defense and transportation in these sea areas. On Wang's Map in this book, 'Korean East Sea' was marked to indicate the sea area east of Korean Peninsula (fig. 1).

<Figure 1> Hai Fang Zuan Yao (海防纂要, Introduction of Coast Defense), by wang zaijin

Wan Li San Da Zheng (万历三大征, Three Expeditions of Emperor Wan Li, 1573-1620) was another book to call this sea area the 'Korean East Sea'. Mao Ruizheng (茅瑞徵), the author, recorded in his three volume work the war between Japan and Korea in 1592. The war, called the 'Korean War during the Wan Li Period' (万历朝鲜之役) in China and 'Defense War in the

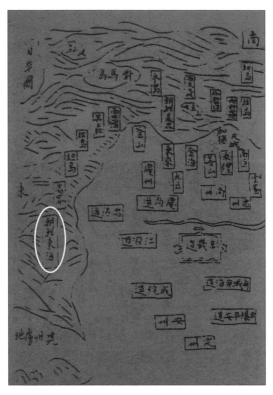

Year of Renchen' (壬辰卫国战争), was triggered by Toyomito Hideyoshi's (丰臣秀吉) invasion to Korean Peninsula. The Ming Government sent troops to the peninsula in response to a request from the Korean king.

After seven years of endeavor, Korea won the war. Mao Ruizheng recorded the war in his book, with some maps to show the battlefield, on which he used the 'Korean East Sea' to

<Figure 2> Wan Li San Da Zheng (万历三大征, Three Expeditions of Emperor Wan Li, 1573-1620), by Mao Ruizheng

indicate the sea area east of the peninsula (fig. 2). In the literature above, the Chinese name for this sea area changed from 'East Sea' to 'Korean East Sea' This might be related with the foundation of Joseon Dynasty of Korea in 1392. During the period, Chinese not only knew more about the sea area but also more about the peninsula.

In conclusion, all the documents and research prove that the name 'East Sea', which originally appeared in Liao and Jin

Dynasty, had been continually used by Nu Zhen and their descendant Manchurian, who lived beside this sea area until the late of Qing Dynasty. After the foundation of the Joseon Dynasty, 'Korean East Sea' appeared in some Chinese literature. Both 'East Sea' and 'Korean East Sea' are names for the same sea areas east of the peninsula, given by the residents living on the western coast of the sea area. The name 'Sea of Japan' by western colonizers in modern history did not have any historical basis. The names recorded in Chinese and Korean historical literature such as 'East Sea' would be the better choice.

Han Maoli

Han Maoli is a professor at the College of Environmental Sciences at Peking University

Russian Geographical Investigations of North-Eastern Asia Seas in XVII-XVIII Centuries [1]

Sergey Ganzey

Since the sixteenth century Russian Cossacks, industrialists, and military men have moved east beyond the Ural mountains to Siberia. Rich new land and the discoveries of unknown spaces attracted them. These lands were colonized and absorbed by Russia. In the seventeenth century, Russian travelers, mainly Cossacks, made many important discoveries, primarily in the eastern and northern part of Asia. The city of Yakutsk became the center of expectations in that century. Russians then began moving from Yakutsk to the south, north, and east to find more new lands. And in 1639 a troop of Cossacks led by Ivan Moskvitin reached the Sea of Okhotsk by the Uile River.

Moskvitin's troops discovered the sea. It was called Lamskoe, from the Tungusic word *laman*, meaning sea or ocean. Later, this body of water was called the Sea of Okhotsk. That name probably is connected with the Okhota River and the Okhotsk berg that the

---

1) This paper has been presented at *The International Workshop on the Geographical Name of 'East Sea'* (1996).

Russians constructed in 1649 near the mouth of the Okhota River. In the eighteenth century, Okhotsk and then the port became bases for important sea expeditions and geographical discoveries. And in 1639 Russians reached the Pacific coast for the first time.

During this period, Russians were beginning to make geographical discoveries for study and for developing the Pacific coast and the seas of northeast Asia. From 1643 to 1646, Cossack troops led by Vasily Pojyarkov traveled from Yakutsk to the Amur River, and sailing along the coastline reached that river's mouth. They next sailed through the Sea of Okhotsk to near Sakhalin. Between 1650 and 1652 Pojyarkov and then Erophey Khabarov investigated and described the coastlines of the Amur River and tribes that lived nearby, such as the Duyger, Gold, Gilyak, and Daur. In 1648 the Russian Cossack Syemyon Dezhnev departed from Kolima and traveled to the extreme northeast of Asia, and for the first time crossed the strait that separates Asia from North America. This strait was later named the Bering Strait. In 1697-1699 Vladimir Atlasov led an expedition, and some of the geographical discoveries and descriptions of Kamchatka are due to him. Atlasov's troops left the Anadir burg and proceeded along the western coast of Kamchatka up to the southern part of the peninsula. Thus by the end of the seventeenth century Russians had collected the first data on the eastern coast of Russia and the adjoining seas to the east and northeast. The discoveries and findings were marked on geographical maps, 'drawings' which were compiled based upon data obtained during these expeditions.

Having been preserved until the present time, these cartographi cal materials of the seventeenth century could not be acknowledged as geographical maps because there was no degree grid. In compiling them, exact measurements were not made.

Nevertheless, these materials show us the level of geographical knowledge typical of that time. The maps or 'drawings' did not provide a real picture of several million square kilometers of territory in Siberia, rivers, and sea coasts.

The 'drawings', compiled in 1667 under Petr Godunov's leadership (Titov, 1890), were among the first cartographical works of that period. The list, attached to Godunov's drawing, describes the route to China, and gives data on several Siberian rivers, including the Amur. Godunov's map shows that the route from the Kolyma River to the Amur River was open. In 1672 a new and more detailed 'Drawing of the Siberian Land' was compiled, but its compiler is not known. Having been completed in 1672, the drawing has A 'List from the Drawing of Siberian Lands' (Titov, 1890) in which the following description is given: "And the Anarur River has two land routes: to the Lama River and to the Bludnaya River. The Bludnaya River entered the Amur River. And the Lama River entered the Amur Sea. The Kolyma River entered the Lenskoye Sea." Here we find one of the first mentions of the name of marine areas east of Siberia. It should be noted that Godunov's drawing showed the Amur River southeast of Siberia.

In 1687, in the book *Noord en Oost Tartarye* (Northern and Eastern Tartary, cited by L.C. Bagrov, 1914) Nic Witsen's map was published. This map was a copy of Godunov's drawing. But we find a number of geographical names of maritime areas on it.

The ocean is called Oceanus Orientalis (Eastern Ocean), and the Amur Sea (as Amur Se Zee) is located opposite the mouth of the Amur River. The Korean Peninsula is shown as an island. The Sea of China (Sinese Zee) is situated to the west and south of the river. Witsen's map was later republished; the name of the waters between Japan and the continent had a double name, Mer Orientale ou Du Japon (fig. 1).

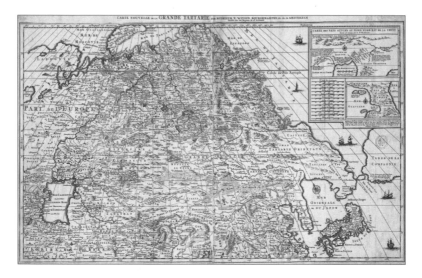

<Figure 1> New Map of Grand Tartarie by N. Witsen (Amsterdam, G. Sanson Publishing House, Russian State Archive of Ancient Acts). Source of Data: *Atlas of the Kurile Islands*. Moscow-Vladivostok, 2009.

Semen Remezov's 'The Drawing Book of Siberia' is the more famous map of that period. Produced in 1690-1700, 'The Drawing Book of Siberia' summarized all geographical materials. This geographical idea was the height of geographical thought in Russia. But many cartographical ideas were not exact and naive. For example, the well-known scientist A.F. Middendorff (1860) remarked, "The boundary lines are combined in the framework of the map itself." The map is oriented to the south. The sea area is shown in the east as a sea-ocean (Akyan). In addition, Kamchatka as an island, Japan (Aponiya) as an island, the Amur River entering the sea (the Amur Sea?), China, and many other geographical features are shown.

<Figure 2> The Map of Tartarie by Abraham Ortelius (Amsterdam, 1570). Source of Data: Atlas of the Kurile Islands. Moscow-Vladivostok, 2009.

It is necessary to mention how the western European geographers of the seventeenth century imagined the seas of East Asia. For example, on the map of Tartarya and Orteliya (or Tatariya, as this name was used for a long period of time for the vast space east of the Urals) that was published in 1570 (fig. 2), the sea between Japan and the continent was marked as Mare CIN, that is, as Sea of China. The same name for this body of water appears in the map of Japan and new islands by Ioann Yanssonii published in Amsterdam in 1658 (fig.3).

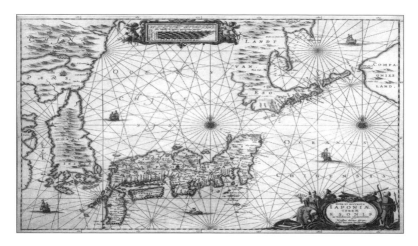

<Figure 3> The Map of Japan and New Islands by Ioann Yanssonii. (Amsterdam, 1658, Collection of Newberry Library, Chicago). Source of Data: *Atlas of the Kurile Islands*. Moscow-Vladivostok, 2009.

Published in 1680, the *History of Siberia* by Yu. Krizhanovich discussed the question of the existence of the strait between the Arctic Sea and the Eastern Sea/Sea of China. In considering this question, we find names for the seas washing Siberia. Thus, data on the names of the seas in East Asia were both common, such as Eastern Sea, Eastern Asia, the Marginal Ocean, and others.

In the second half of the seventeenth century Nikolai Spaphary (1675-1678), a Russian diplomat, made a trip that was very important because it formed new ideas in geography. He wrote about the borders of China, stating that beyond China to the east is a very large island. The distance between this island and the

Chinese border is about 700 versts (8 verst is 3,500 feet. This term is translated from Old Russian). Its name is Japoniya, and this island has more riches than China. From the results of his travels Spaphary prepared the book *The Description of the First Part of the Earth called Asia, the Chinese Kingdom with Other Cities and Provinces* (1677, cited by Lebedev, 1949). Spaphary touched upon questions about the geographical location of China. He also provided characteristics of parts of the world, such as Asia, Europe, Liviya, and America.

Further, it is said that the eastern part Asia is separated from the other parts of the world by the Eastern Sea, and in the north only by the Ocean Arctic Sea, and from midday (noon)-by the Indian and Black Sea. In another publication, *The Narration about the Great Amur River that Divides the Russian Settlement with China,* Spaphary acknowledged that it was possible to sail south from the Amur River. He wrote, "One can go from Amur to China. But it is very far. It is necessary to go round the great nose of Korea which extends to the sea." (Lebedev, 1949) Spaphary's evidence was very important for further geographical studies of the East Asian seas in Russia because at that time the fundamental strategic goal of the Russian government was to solve two objectives: to find ways to reach North America and to find a sea route to China and India.

Russian geographical studies of the seventeenth century were connected with the activity of two great rulers, Peter the First (1682-1725) and Ekaterina the Great (1729-1796). By the early seventeenth century Russia had found routes to the Baltic Sea, which strengthened the country's economic ties with Western Europe. Peter the First frequently dreamed of finding the routes to India, China, Japan, and North America. G. Perry, an Englishman who worked in Russia, heard many times how the czar expressed his wish "to send people to draw a true map in order to determine if it is possible for ships to pass near New Zealand and reach the Sea of Tatar in the east. [...] There one could build ships to sail to the Chinese and Japanese shores." Peter the First was eager to learn how far the Far Eastern lands extended and whether they were open to capture.

Expeditions in the first half of the seventeenth century were very important. In 1700 Michail Nasedkin discovered that there is land to the south of Kamchatka, behind the strait. This led to an expedition in 1711-1713 organized by Danil Antsipherov. This project investigated some northern Kurile Islands. In 1715-1717 the maritime expedition headed by Kuzma Sokolov investigated the western part of Kamchatka and reached Okhotsk by sea for the first time. From then on there were regular sea trips from Okhotsk to Kamchatka. In 1725-1743 Vitus Bering organized an expedition. Before his death, Peter the First wrote instructions addressed to Bering in which he instructed the expedition to determine whether there is a strait between Asia and North America. As a result of the first Siberian-Pacific expedition (1725-1730), Bering proceeded along the eastern coast of the Chukotka Peninsula by the strait which later was named for him, and opened the Krest Gulf, Provedeniya Bay, and St. Diomid Island. In 1727 another expedition was organized by A. Shestakov and D. Prelutsky. Its goal was to determine if it was possible to sail from the Arctic Ocean to the Eastern Sea. To find a way to Japan from the mouth of the Amur River was another goal discussed in the course of its formation. During this expedition, though, Shestakov passed away. G. Fedorov and M. Gvozdev continued the expedition in 1730, and became the first Russians, in 1732, to reach the North American coast. The first map of the Bering Strait was compiled from their materials.

To confirm the results of the first Bering expedition and those of Fedorov and Gvozdev (that is, the existence of the strait which unites the Northern and Eastern seas, and to search for the shortest route to Japan and the establishment of friendly relationships between Russia and Japan) the second Siberian-Pacific (Kamchatka) expedition was organized by the Russian government (1733-1741). At that time Russia and western countries knew little about the outlines of Japan. East of the island of Iezo (Ezo, Hokkaido), Matmai, a large island of states was known. Further to the east, Gammi is shown (Beiker, 1950). According to information from a Dutch traveler who visited this area in the seventeenth century, these lands were very rich. Further, Iezo was often united with Asia and North America on maps. The second Siberian-Pacific expedition was divided into two groups: Bering and A. Chirikov investigated the route to North America, and M. Shpanberg's group investigated the route from Kamchatka to Japan (Berg, 1946).

The expedition headed by Bering and Chirikov began in 1734, traveling from Yakutsk to Okhotsk. But only in 1740 did they manage to reach the sea and sail to Kamchatka. In 1741 they left the eastern shores of Kamchatka (from Avachinskaya Bay), went to North America, and reached the shores of Alaska. Conditions for this expedition were extremely difficult. Many people died of disease, including Bering in 1741. During this expedition, the Bering Strait and the northeastern coasts of North America – Alaska, the Aleutian Islands, and Bering Island – were discovered for the second time after Dezhnev. Drawings of the Sea of Okhotsk's shores were made. In 1739-1742, Shpanberg's detachment investigated and mapped the Kurile Islands and a part of Sakhalin island, and traveled along the eastern coast of Sakhalin. Finally, for the first time Shpanberg's expedition found the route to Japan from the north, and proved that Gama Land did not exist and that State Island and Companiya Land are two islands in the Kurile range. In the second half of the seventeenth century, after the second Siberian-Pacific expedition, Russian studies concentrated on the description of the Alaskan shores. The Aleutian and Komandor islands can be explained by the active development of Russian America. Krenitsin and Levashov's expeditions to the Aleutian Islands were the largest of that period. In 1791 Bocharov described the northern shore of the Alaskan peninsula. In 1790-1792 L.A. Sarichev (1802) described the Aleutian, Komandar, and other islands in the Bering Sea. The maps of seas of East Asia were based on the rich materials from these Russian expeditions. In 1701 the drawing (fig.4) of Kamchatka, the Kurile Islands, and Japan (Lebedev, 1949) was made by C.I. Remezov. Unfortunately, this drawing does not contain geographical names. It only gives a general picture and shows that at the beginning of the eighteenth century Russian investigators thought that Kamchatka was a peninsula and that the Kurile Islands and Japan were located south of Kamchatka. In 1713 the map of Asia by B.O. Kupriyanov appeared (Ephimov, 1950), on which Iedso was shown and the sea was called the Western Ocean?!

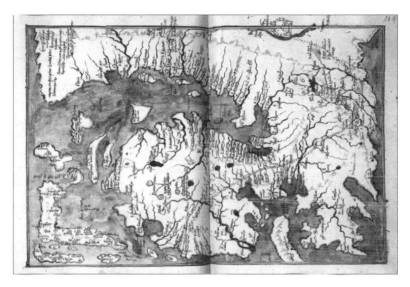

<Figure 4> The Drawing of the Kamchatka and Northeast Extreme end of Asia by Semen Remesov, 1701. (Russian Scientific Library). Source of Data: *Atlas of the Kurile Islands*. Moscow-Vladivostok, 2009.

In 1724 I.K. Kirilov (Lebedev, 1950) compiled a map called "A Map of the Geographical Area of Far Eastern Siberia and Tatariya," with new lands of Kamchatka and Japan based on the maps compiled by geodesists Ivan Evreinov and Fedor Luzhin, whom Peter the Great had sent in 1719 to determine if Asia and North America adjoin each other. Later, after discussions with I. Shestacov, whose map was very popular, Kirilov's map was supplemented

(Ephimov, 1950). These maps showed the outlines of Kamchatka better than other maps, but the Kurile Islands, Sakhalin, and northern Japan were depicted rather roughly. The comment written on the map, in the sea dividing Japan and the Korean Peninsula, is worth noting: "The shore of the Kingdom (state?) called Korea. To the Amur River was copied from Chinese maps."

In 1723 Goman's *Atlas* was published (Lebedev, 1950). This text showed the territory from Chukotka to Japan (fig. 5). The sea, situated north of Sakhalin, was called Lamskoye, Penzhinskoe Sea. The sea located in the southern and eastern part of Sakhalin is called Eastern Ocean. Later, in 1759, this map was produced again (Ephimov, 1950) and called 'The Newest Outlines of Asia'. It shows three names – Lamskoye, Penzhinskoye Sea, and Meridional Sea[Mare Meridionale] – for the present Sea

<Figure 5> The Map of Kamchatka and Jedso by I.B. Homann, 1723. (From the collection of A.M. Bulatov, Moscow). Source of Data: *Atlas of the Kurile Islands*. Moscow-Vladivostok, 2009.

of Okhotsk. In the east, along the Japanese islands, is Marginal Japanese Sea and in the waters east of the islands is Eastern 'Sea of Japan.' In 1733 I. Kirilov prepared 'A General Map of Russia' (*Atlas of Geographical Discoveries in the 17th-18th Centuries*, 1964), which was then published in 1734. In the south and the east, waters are called the Eastern Ocean (fig. 6). East of Iezo Land (Hokkaido) is Companiya Land, and further to the east is Gama Land, though the expeditions organized by Bering and Chirikov and by Shpanberg had proven that Gama did not exist. In 1742 V.I. Kazantsev compiled the handmade map 'Penzhinskoye Sea from Okhotsk to Great River and Kamchadaliya' (Ephimov, 1950). On this map are Penzhinskoye Sea, North America, and Japan. The sea located south of the Amur River is called Japponiya.

As for cartographic ideas about East Asia, there were contradictions between Russian and Western European cartographers. Seuter's map of Russia published in 1739 may serve as an example of such a contradiction (the

<Figure 6> General Map of the Russian Empire by Ivan Kirillov, 1734 (Russian State Library). Source of Data: *Atlas of the Kurile Islands*. Moscow-Vladivostok, 2009.

map is presented in Bagrov, 1914). For example, the Sea of Japan is situated in the present Bering Sea, Sakhalin is located further north than the Amur River; and the sea between the Korean Peninsula, Japan, and Kamchatka is occupied by Kamchatka Bay. On the basis of the Russian expeditions in the first part of the eighteenth century the Russian Academy of Science published the *Atlas of Russia* in 1745. A general map of the Russian Empire is attached to this *Atlas*. On the spot of the present Sea of Okhotsk is Kamchatkoe Sea; east of Kamchatka is Pacific Ocean; east of Sakhalin along the coast of present Primorskii Krai is Pacific Sea.

It is necessary to note that the terms Eastern Ocean, Pacific Ocean, Eastern Sea, and Pacific Sea are often used as synonyms in the geographical literature of that period. A general map of the Russian Empire was republished in 1787 (fig. 7). It is interesting to

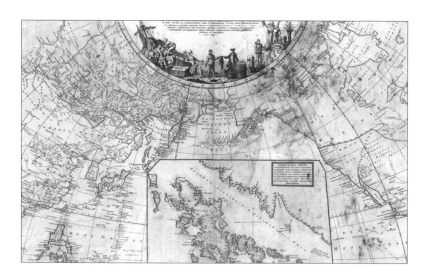

<Figure 7> The General Map of the Russian Empire, 1787. Source of Data: *Atlas of the Kurile Islands*. Moscow-Vladivostok, 2009.

note that the sea between Japan and Korea was called Korean Sea. As for the maps of the second part of the seventeenth century, we can cite only 'The Map of the Irkutsk Government, 1796' (fig. 8), on which Okhotskoe Sea and Korean Sea are shown.

Russian cartographers of the eighteenth century often showed the seas occupied by the present Sea of Okhotsk and Bering Sea on their maps. The sea located south of Sakhalin and between the Japanese islands and the continent was not of great interest. At that time the boundary between the Russian Empire and China was drawn at approximately 55°N and in the east at approximately 140°E. In 1771 the concrete name Sea of Korea is given to this sea. We found this in *Encyclopedia Britannica*. This name was widely used by the Russian geographers who investigated East Asia. V.M. Golovnin (1972) described his adventures in his notes when he

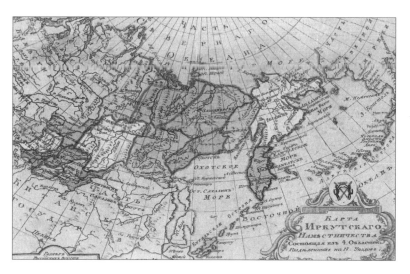

<Figure 8> The Map of Irkutsk Government (Russian State Archive of Ancient Acts). Source of Data: *Atlas of the Kurile Islands*. Moscow-Vladivostok, 2009.

was captured and held as a prisoner by Japanese in 1811, 1812, and 1813. He wrote (p. 39), "On August 6, 1792, they left Avachin Guba. They intend to describe the Korean Sea and went southwest along the Kurile range. But because of the fog, they did not manage to see land until August 20. It was too late, and they could not describe the Korean Sea and had to come back." After the French traveler La Pérouse crossed the strait for the first time, he called the Korean Sea as the Tatar Sea. Today, the strait is named after him.

Thus, in the eighteenth century the geographical names of the Russian Far East reflected the complex period of geographical studies and development of these vast marine spaces. At different times in the eighteenth century the Bering Sea was called Pacific, Eastern, Japanese, and Anadir. The modern Sea of Okhotsk also had many names in the eighteenth century, such as Lamskoye, Penzhinskoye, Kamchatka Bay, and Okhotskoe. The part of the sea near the mouth of the Amur River was called Amur Sea. The history of the name for the sea that divides Japan and the continent is not simple. At different times in the eighteenth century this sea was called Eastern, Pacific, Chinese, Tatar, Japan, Marginal Japanese, 'Sea of Japan', and Sea of Korea. From early on vast Russian-American colonies were established through Siberia and Okhotsk, and these brought various difficulties. Therefore, it was decided to supply the colonies by sea. As a result, at the beginning of the nineteenth century expeditions to sail around the world were organized, the first by I.F. Kruzenshtem and Yu. F. Lisyansky in 1803-1805. They started in Kronshtadt (St. Petersburg). One of the expedition's tasks was to take the Russian embassy to Japan in order to establish trade relations with that country. The embassy was not accepted by Japan. Kruzenshtern's expedition followed La Pérouse's route along the eastern shores of Japan and the southern coast of Sakhalin, and then crossed the La Pérouse Strait.

In 1813, as a result of the expedition, the *Atlas* was published (*Atlas*, 1813). Later, in 1826, G.I. Sarichev's 'The Atlas of the Northern Part of the Eastern Ocean' was published. Compiled based upon the results of Kruzenshtem's voyage, it includes a map of the Pacific. The Anadir Sea is marked in the northern part of the Bering Sea and the Sakhalin Sea is shown in the southern part of the Sea of Okhotsk, along the eastern coast of Sakhalin. The sea between Japan and the continent is called 'Sea of Japan'. In the northern part of this sea is shown the Tatar Strait, whereas Sakhalin is depicted as a peninsula. In 1849 this mistake was corrected by G.I. Nevelskoy's investigations. He proved that there was a strait between Sakhalin and the mainland (1878). On all later Russian geographical maps the sea to the west of Japan is called Sea of Japan.

Conclusion

Every sea of Eastern Russia can pretend to different names. For example, the Sea of Okhotsk can be called either Kamchatskoye Sea or Lamskoye Sea. But for about two hundred years, from 1650-1850, Okhotsk was the main port from which Russian geographical expeditions started. Therefore, the name Sea of Okhotsk is more supported by history. The Bering Sea also had multiple names, such as Kamchatskoye, Pacific, and Bobrovoye.

But Vitus Bering solved one of the important problems, one which had existed for several centuries in Russia and Europe. He discovered the marine route from northeast Asia to North America and proved the existence of the strait between Asia and North America that enabled his followers to rename that body of water as Kamchatskoye Sea. Today it is called the Bering Sea. The 'Sea of Japan' has had different names, too, such as Eastern, Korean, Pacific, Tatar, and Japanese. But despite the use of 'Sea of Japan' since the nineteenth century, that name has been used in the Russian geographical literature from an earlier period. We believe that this can be explained by the long isolation of Japan and by the fact that Japan did not wish to establish trade relations with Russia or other European countries. At the same time it was thought that this country had great riches beyond those of China. It was 'Eastern India' in people's dreams. The frequent attempts to reach this country were unsuccessful. These facts apparently influenced the Russian geographers to use the name Sea of Japan for that body of water opening the way to Japan.

Note: *The author thanks the Society of Study of Amurskyi Krai (Vladivostok) for the opportunity to work in the library and archives of the Society.*

REFERENCES

Atlas of Captain Kruzenshtem's Travel around the World (1813), St. Petersburg.

Atlas of the Kurile Islands (2009), Moscow-Vladivostok.

Atlas of the Northern Part of the Eastern Ocean (1826), St. Petersburg.

Bagrov, L.S. *Maps of Asian Russia* (1914), Petrograd.

Berg, L.S. (1926), *Pacific Ocean*, 1-24, Russian Scientific Studies, Moscow.

Berg, L.S. (1946), *Notes about the History of Russian Geographic Discoveries.* Moscow-Leningrad, AS USSR.

Beiker, G. (1950), *History of Geographical Discoveries.* Moscow, Foreign Literature.

Deeds of Russian Marine Officers in the Extreme Russian Far East 1849-1855: PreAmurskyi Krai, PreUssuriyskyi Krai. Posthumous notes written by Admiral Nevelskoy (1878), St. Petersburg.

Ephimov, A.V. (1950), *From the History of Great Russian Geographic Discoveries in the Arctic and Pacific Oceans.* The Seventeenth and the First Part of the Eighteenth Centuries. Moscow, Geographgiz.

Lebedev, D.M. (1949), *Geography in Russia in the Seventeenth Century* (Pre-Peter the First Epoch), Moscow-Leningrad, AS USSR.

Lebedev, D.M. (1950), *Geography in Russia in the Peter the First Period.* Moscow-Leningrad, AS USSR.

Magidovich, I.P. (1967), *Notes about the History of Geographic*

Discoveries. Moscow, Prosveshchenie.

Middendorff, A.F., Travels to Northern and Eastern Siberia, part 1. St. Petersburg.

Notes of Captain I. Golovnin (1972), Fleet about his Adventures When he was a Prisoner in Japan in 1811, 1812, and 1813. Khabarovsk.

Perri, G. (1871), *The State in Russia Headed by the Present Czar.* Moscow.

Sarichev, G,A. (1952), Travels of Captain Sarichev's Fleet along the Northeastern Part of Siberia, the Arctic Ocean, and the Eastern Sea during Eight Years, Organized by Geographical and Astronomic Marine Expedition under the Leadership of Captain Billings from 1785 to 1793, parts I and II. St. Petersburg, 1902, New edition, Moscow.

Titov, A. (1890), Siberia in the Seventeenth Century. Moscow.

Sergey Ganzey

Sergey Ganzey is deputy director at the Pacific Institute of Geography that belongs to the Far Eastern Branch of the Russian Academy of Sciences. He is vice chairman at the International Geographical Union Commission on Land Use/Cover Change. He has experience in conducting and coordinating transboundary diagnostic analysis projects.

International Framework

United Nations Resolutions on Maritime Feature Names

Peter E. Raper

Abstract

Since time immemorial people have referred to seas and oceans by names in their own language. The proliferation of maritime features is sometimes problematical in international contexts, leading to confusion and perhaps even conflict. In terms of its Charter, the mission of the United Nations is to maintain world peace, develop good relations between conturies, promote co-operation in solving the world's problems, and encourage respect for human rights.[1] United Nations resolutions are specifically drafted, adopted and ratified to achieve these aims. The resolutions are effective in their recognition of the national sovereignty of countries in the standardization of geographical names, and may be useful in covering the eventuality of names of maritime features that fall beyond the sovereignty of any one nation. A solution is proposed whereby the sovereignty of each country is extended to include names of maritime features beyond its territorial waters, so as to reduce the number and impact of feature names which fall outside any jurisdiction and are therefore susceptible to dispute.

---

1) United Nations, *Microsoft® Encarta® Encyclopedia 99.*© 1993-1998 Microsoft Corporation. All rights reserved.

Ⅰ. Introduction

Geographical names, also called place-names or toponyms, are among the oldest words in any language. Since people first began to communicate with each other, they gave names to features on land, and also to water features such as seas, oceans and their sub-divisions, and to undersea features. Because people in different parts of the world, and even in the same country, speak different languages and dialects, the same feature sometimes has names in different languages. Thus, for example, the Black Sea is also known as *Cherno More* (Bulgarian), *Chernoye More* (Russian), *Kara Deniz* (Turkish), *Marea Neagra* (Romanian), *Mer Noire* (French), *Mustameri* (Finnish), *Swart See* (Afrikaans), *Zwart Zee* (Dutch), *Schwarzes Meer* (German), and *Euxine Sea* (English).

The same situation potentially exists for the name of every sea and ocean in the world. Every maritime feature in the world has names from different languages when referred to by people speaking different languages. People have the right to refer to such a feature by a name in their own language. However, when various names compete at an international level, the potential is sometimes strong for misunderstanding, confusion and even conflict.

Ⅱ. The United Nations

The primary purpose of the United Nations – and the greatest benefit to its members – is to maintain world peace and avoid conflict between nations. The United Nations provides a forum for countries to promote their views and settle conflicts without violence, and promotes and coordinates economic and social progress in developing countries (Microsoft Encarta Encyclopedia 99).

At an early stage the United Nations identified geographical names as one of the areas most likely to cause conflict, and accordingly established the United Nations Group of Experts on Geographical Names (UNGEGN) to advise it in this regard. The UNGEGN consists of experts in linguistics, cartography and other subjects relevant to geographical names, and is the most authoritative body on Earth for the standardization of geographical names.

A geographical name is a: "Name applied to a feature on the surface of the Earth (Kadmon et al. 1996:137)." A feature is "A portion of the surface of the Earth... that has recognizable identity." By standardization is understood "the prescription by a names authority of one or more particular names, together with their precise written form, for application to a given geographical feature, as well as the conditions for their use (Kadmon 1996:144)."

At United Nations Conferences on the Standardization of Geographical Names, which are held every five years, issues relating to geographical names are discussed, problems are identified and solutions sought. Resolutions are drafted and adopted, the implementation of which leads to effective communication, with resultant economic and social benefits.

At the First United Nations Conference on the Standardization of Geographical Names, held in Geneva in 1967, it was recognized that each country has the sovereign prerogative to standardize the geographical names under its jurisdiction, that is, to decide on the name of every feature, and how that name should be written. The relevant resolution also recommends that the geographical names standardized by each country should be disseminated as widely as possible, and be used by other countries. International standardization of geographical names must thus be based on national standardization.

At this First Conference, it was noted that a lack of uniformity in the naming by different countries of maritime features, and also of undersea features, was adversely affecting the safety of navigation. The sovereign right of each country to standardize the geographical names under its jurisdiction includes the names of maritime features. According to the Law of the Sea(1994), "jurisdiction refers to the power of a state to affect persons, property and circumstances within its territory," and that includes its maritime zones (Kadmon 2007:2). Each state thus has authority to confer maritime names, which come under the term 'circumstances' as stipulated in the Law, over those parts of the sea that fall under the definition of 'territorial waters (Kadmon 2007:2~3)'.

According to the charts of the International Hydrographic Bureau, each country has territorial waters 12 nautical miles in extent under its jurisdiction, measured from the low-water baselines. Beyond the territorial waters the sea to a distance of 24 nautical miles from the baselines are the Contiguous and Maritime Cultural Zones of the country. The sea beyond the Territorial Waters to a distance of 200 nautical miles is the Exclusive Economic Zone. Beyond these limits are international waters, falling beyond the jurisdiction of any one country, and sometimes called the high seas (Möller 1999:181).

Ⅲ. Co-operation with Relevant Bodies

Since the necessity of cooperation with other relevant bodies was realized, the United Nations Group of Experts strove to implement the adopted resolutions in this regard, and the following progress was made.

- In pursuance of Resolution 8 of the First Conference, the United Nations Group of Experts on Geographical Names obtained from the Intergovernmental Oceanographic Commission(IOC), the International Hydrographic Bureau(IHB) and the International Association of Physical Oceanography(IAPO), full particulars of the work already accomplished by those organizations, and continued to consult with and, as appropriate, to use the facilities of these bodies to further United Nations objectives in international standardization of names of maritime and undersea features.
- In pursuance of Resolution 22 of the Second U.N. Conference, the United Nations Group of Experts on Geographical Names

studied existing national and international practices concerning the delimitation and naming of oceans and seas, including their integral subdivisions, beyond the limits of national jurisdiction, with a view to recommending improvements in current nomenclatural practices and procedures.

• By the year 1977, when the Third Conference was held, cognizance had been taken that the International Hydrographic Organization had designated a technical committee to recommend improvements in procedures for naming oceans and seas and their integral subdivisions – referred to as maritime features – beyond the limits of national jurisdiction.

•In pursuance of Resolution 21 of the Third Conference, the United Nations Group of Experts on Geographical Names accepted the offer of the International Hydrographic Association to assist in United Nations programs related to maritime features, and coordinated its programs with those of the International Hydrographic Organization.

• In pursuance of Resolution 12 of the Fourth Conference, work in maritime features was further coordinated with similar work of the International Hydrographic Office, as recommended by the Third United Nations Conference on the Standardization of Geographical Names in its Resolution 21, and the Group of Experts identified a point of contact to carry out essential liaison and communications regarding names of undersea features proposed by national bodies.

Ⅳ. Features over More than One Sovereignty

In some cases a feature may extend over more than one sovereignty, or be shared by more than one country. The names of these features cannot then be decided upon by any one nation, and their standardization requires co-operation between countries and organizations.

To make provision for such eventualities, Resolution 8 of the First Conference set the stage for a series of subsequent resolutions that provide guidance in such cases. It reads as follows:

The Conference,

Recognizing that some features common to, or extending across the frontiers of, two or more nations have more than one name applied to them,

Further recognizing that the names of some features of this kind have different applications or extent,

1. Considers that it is preferable that a common name or a common application be established, wherever practicable, in the interest of international standardization;

2. Recommends that the geographical names authorities of the nations concerned attempt to reach agreement on these conflicting names or applications.

In the following conferences, further resolutions in this regard were adopted. Resolution 20 of the Third Conference reads:

The Conference,

Considering the need for international standardization of names of geographical features that are under the sovereignty of more than one country or are divided among two or more countries,

1. Recommends that countries sharing a given geographical feature under different names should endeavor, as far as possible, to reach agreement on fixing a single name for the feature concerned;

2. Further recommends that when countries sharing a given geographical feature do not succeed in agreeing on a common name, it should be a general rule of international cartography that the name used by each of the countries concerned will be accepted. A policy of accepting only one or some of such names while excluding the rest would be inconsistent in principle as well as inexpedient in practice. Only technical reasons may sometimes make it necessary, especially in the case of small-scale maps, to dispense with the use of certain names belonging to one language or another.

Finally, Resolution 25 of the Fifth Conference was adopted, reading as follows:

The Conference,

Considering that it would be useful to know and compare the practical experience acquired by neighboring countries in the standardization of names of geographical features extending across their common borders,

1. Recommends that Member States systematically inform future United Nations conferences on the standardization of geographical names of their achievements in this field;
2. Recommends to that end that those national geographical names authorities that have not yet done so establish with neighboring authorities joint or interrelated programs for the collection and treatment of names of features extending across their common borders.

Ⅴ. International Waters

Most of the Earth's maritime features fall beyond the sovereignty of any one nation or country. These features are, in other words, international waters or 'high seas'. Such features "can carry any name applied to them by different linguistic or political communities such as different countries. By 'carrying' a name is meant its being used on the one hand in written verbal documents, such as in literature and particularly in geographical gazetteers and indexes, and on the other hand in maps and maritime charts (Kadmon 2007:3)." As already noted above, most maritime features have different names in different languages, known as alternative names or allonyms. To achieve international standardization of names of international waters, the United Nations Group of Experts on Geographical Names at the outset established a Working Group on Maritime and Undersea Feature Names, which co-operated with the International Hydrographic Organization (IHO). The IHO published a list of maritime names under the title Limits of Oceans and Seas, the first edition of which had been published in 1929 as Special Publication 23. It was agreed to accept the names given for international waters by the IHO for the purposes of international standardization, and to encourage all countries to use these names (Kadmon 2000:224). As has emerged subsequently, however, not all countries were in a position to participate in the recommendations and decisions at the time, and an attempt to update the publication in 2007 and subsequently has proven to be problematic, and is still being deliberated upon.

Ⅵ. Extension of National Jurisdiction

Resolution 4 of the First United Nations Conference on the Standardization of Geographical Names that recommends the national standardization of geographical names has been successfully implemented in many countries. National names authorities of one kind or another have been established, standardization programs undertaken and standardized names disseminated. The principle of national sovereignty has proved to be successful and effective in ensuring optimal social and economic benefits. In furthering the aims of the United Nations to the benefit of all countries, the extension of national sovereignty, with a concomitant reduction of contentious geographical features, is advocated. This may be achieved by extending the principle of national sovereignty to include maritime features beyond the 12 nautical miles limits of territorial waters, namely those in the Contiguous and Maritime Cultural Zones to a distance of 24 nautical miles from the baselines of the country, and in the Exclusive Economic Zone to a distance of 200 nautical miles beyond the Territorial Waters.

By extending the jurisdiction of each country in this way, each country concerned will have equal say over the names in such areas and zones. Nationally standardized names of the features in the extended areas will then be the official endonyms, while other names for these features will be exonyms. National standardization of these names will thus make possible and facilitate the reduction or elimination of exonyms as recommended by United Nations resolutions.

If the body of water between two countries is less than 400 nautical miles, and application of the principle under discussion results in an overlap of jurisdiction, the meeting-point of the extended limit of each country may be the dividing line, so that each country has an equal distance from its base-line under its jurisdiction. If the body of water between the two countries is more than 400 nautical miles, the features falling beyond the extended national jurisdiction of each country will be in international waters.

The UNGEGN Working Group on Evaluation and Implementation, in collaboration with the Scientific Committee on Undersea Feature Names, the Intergovernmental Oceanographic Commission, the International Hydrographic Bureau, the International Association of Physical Oceanography, the International Hydrographic Organization and other relevant organizations, may wish to consider submitting a draft resolution in this regard to the next U.N. Conference on the Standardization of Geographical Names. The adoption and implementation of such a resolution would increase the jurisdiction of each country, reduce the number of maritime feature names open to arbitrary nomenclature, and reduce the potential for dispute and conflict.

Ⅶ. Draft Resolution

Maritime and undersea features

The Conference,

Noting the success of the standardization of geographical names based on the principle of national sovereignty;

Considering that the elimination of ambiguity regarding the names of maritime and undersea features can be achieved by acknowledging national sovereignty in a greater number of instances;

Recommends that names of maritime and undersea features falling within the Exclusive Economic Zone on a country be recognized as falling under the jurisdiction of that country also for the purposes of geographical name standardization;

Further recommends that in relevant cases the limits of the continental shelf be considered for utilization in a similar fashion;

Recommends also that a UNGEGN working group be established to investigate and make recommendations concerning the standardization of maritime and undersea features falling beyond any national sovereignty, involving consultation with relevant bodies including the Scientific Committee on Undersea Feature Names, the Intergovernmental Oceanographic Commission, the International Hydrographic Bureau, the International Association of Physical Oceanography, and the International Hydrographic Organization.

REFERENCES

Cherkis, Norman Z. (2007), Toponymy and undersea topographic features. *The 13ᵗʰ International Seminar on the Naming of Sea and 'East Sea'*. Vienna : University of Vienna, pp. 65-99.

International Hydrographic Organization (1953), *Limits of Oceans and Sea ; Special Publication No.23*. Monaco : International Hydrographic Organization.

Kadmon, Naftali (2000), *Toponymy : the Lore, Laws and Language of Geographical Names*. New York : Vantage Press.

Kadmon, Naftali (2007), Nihon Kae and Tong Hae - 'Sea of Japan' and 'East Sea' : are they exonyms or allonyms, and is there a missing term? *The 13ᵗʰ International Seminar on the Naming of Sea and 'East Sea'*. Vienna : University of Vienna, pp.1-5.

Kim, Shin (2007), The change of hydrographic environment and Special Publication 23. *The 13ᵗʰ International Seminar on the Naming of Seas and 'East Sea'*. Vienna : University of Vienna, pp. 135-148.

Lee, Ki-Suk and Möller L.A. (comp) (2002), *UNGEGN Statutes, Rules of Procedure and Resolutions on Geographical Names*. Seoul : Working Group on Evaluation and Implementation.

Microsoft Encarta Encyclopedia (1999), Microsoft Corporation. Möller, Lucie (1999), Progress on naming issues in South Africa : who looks out to sea? In : *The Fifth International Seminar on the Naming of Seas*. Seoul : Ministry of

Government Administration and Home Affairs.

Raper, P.E. (comp) (1996), *United Nations Documents on Geographical Names*. Pretoria : Names Research Institute.

Raper, P.E. (ed) (2004), *United Nations Resolutions on Geographical Names Arranged Alphabetically by Subject*. Pretoria : Names Research Institute.

Raper, Peter E. (2007), United Nations resolutions pertaining to the names of seas and oceans. *The 13ᵗʰ International Seminar on the Naming of Seas and 'East Sea'*. Vienna : University. pp. 246-280.

Peter E. Raper

Peter E. Raper was a former chairman of the United Nations Group of Experts on Geographical Names and has served as a research associate at the Department of Language Management and Language Practice at the University of the Free State, Bloemfontein, South Africa

Problematic of the Appellations of the Names of the Seas and Oceans and Policies of the UNGEGN [1]

Brahim Atoui

Preamble

In this paper we will try on the one hand to recall succinctly the role and the objectives of the United Nations Group of Experts on Geographical Names(UNGEGN) as well as its recommendations with regard to the 'Sea of Japan', and on the other hand to treat the problem of the denomination of the seas and oceans. Also, we will attempt to raise the legitimacy of the antecedence of the appellations and the problem of the support of diffusion of the toponyms, notably cartographic support, as a determining tool in their diffusion and promotion at the national and at the international level.

---

1) This paper has been presented at *The 9th International Seminar on the Naming of Seas* (2008).

I. Introduction

The names of places have always constituted, and certainly will constitute for a long time, political stakes of great importance. It is no less important that these must be the factors of proximity and understanding between the different peoples and nations of the world and not only parameters of litigation and confrontation. This is one of the goals for which the UNGEGN was created in 1959. It is in this sense that the UNGEGN does not stop actively promoting the normalization of geographical names in international and national contexts, and thus contributes to better understanding among peoples.

II. The Problem of the Denominations of Seas and Oceans

If it is accepted that the name of a place is an element bearing weight and an important cultural message, it is also one of the most meaningful markers of the belonging of this named space because to name a space means to take possession of it. A place only exists if it is named. The name of a place plays a cultural role and a technical role at the same time, compared to the other information that it conveys. It is for this reason that place names are seen in so many civilizations and nations, and compose part of the heritage of a country.

What explains why countries are very protective of their toponymy? If naming a terrestrial place posed no problem to our predecessors, it is not the same for the seas and the oceans. The denomination of these bodies of water was on the one hand given very late. On the other hand, these bodies constitute by definition liquid spaces which are therefore changing and moving. Further, these spaces have surfaces which are poorly defined, are surrounded by but little land, are poorly known, are sometimes feared, and are therefore difficult to name with precision.

Man did not feel the need to name maritime spaces until it was too late. That is to say, these spaces were not named until he began to travel the seas and the oceans in search of other civilizations, other continents, and other needs. In their quest of discovery, the first pioneers, while establishing the first maritime maps of discovered maritime spaces, have sought more so to produce maps of these spaces without insisting too much on their appellations. The first maps only included very few toponyms. They reported the names of beaches, islands, and straits, but only a very few names of seas.

Thereafter, with the continuation of discoveries and the impli-cation of numerous nations in the research of new continents and new wealth, notably from the eighteenth century, denomi-nation became more an act of demand and of appropriation. It is in this context that most of these spaces came to be named. The established maps included the new assigned names and a few former autochthonous names. These latter names typically were transcribed according to the subtleties of the discoverer's language, and were at the same time 'nationalized'.

If in an earlier time the assignment of names to places was not the responsibility of the political authorities, the denominations resulted from a convenient, spontaneous and, in particular, oral use. Henceforth, with the arrival of these newcomers, some of the names will be 'politicized' and transcribed forever under one form or another. They will thereafter be connected to another civilization, and will glorify and honor some individuals and perpetuate their memory. Such individuals notably were the discoverers of a passage, a sea, or an island. Pérouse, Berrine, and others are examples.

The peoples of non-maritime traditions, that "turned their back to the sea," have been subjected to more prejudice as regards their toponymic heritage. People of East Asia are an example. The Chinese maps of Asia for example did not include names of seas, 'without exception'.[2] This absence of appellations for the seas is especially meaningful as Chinese tradition recommended not only the correct transcription of the names of places but insisted also already on their 'normalization', that is, the writing of the names of places in a correct form and on the political stake that the denominations constitute.

Confucius recommended 500 years before Jesus Christ "to return to every thing its true name" and :

If the names do not suit the things, there is confusion. If there is confusion, the things do not execute themselves. If the things do not execute themselves, decorum and harmony are

---

2) See Pelletier, Philippe (2000), Tumulte of the Streams between Japan and Korea, about the Denomination of 'Sea of Japan', *Annals of Geography* 613. pp. 279-305.

disregarded. Decorum being disregarded, the torments and the other punishments are not proportional to the mistakes. The torments and the other punishments not being proportional anymore to the mistakes, the people do not know anymore where to put the hand or the foot.

Did the few denominations of maritime spaces in the East Asian region mean that the seas were not yet considered as places? Because they were not frequented and therefore of no utility, and thus not named.

Ⅲ. What Appellation? East Sea? Sea of Japan? Sea of China? Sea of Korea? Another?: Antecedence of the Appellations and the Legitimacy of Cartographic Support

The literature treating the history and the problems of the appellation of seas is abundant. I will thus bring practically no contribution to this topic. Nevertheless, my contribution will center on the problem of the legitimacy of the antecedence of the appellations as a determining factor, as well as in the demand for and the consecration of the toponym on the national level and on the international level.

If we conduct a retrospective study of the denomination of this sea, what should we note? We note that the first time before the sixteenth century the tools of diffusion and promotion of the toponyms, that is, maps, written works, and orally transmitted information, are rare, but that the most wide spread and the most cited support is maps. Before the sixteenth century, we note that two known maps, one Chinese and the other Korean, included the appellation of this sea.[3] On one map it is identified as Sea of Korea, and on the other map as 'East Sea'.

The toponym 'Sea of Japan' first appears in international cartography in European maps.[4] Is European cartographic support the principal reference and does it enjoy the necessary credibility?

Ⅳ. Duality of the Appellations

It is from the arrival of the Europeans and their important cartographic production, notably the map of the world by Matteo Ricci (1552-1610), that the duality and the competition between the different appellations makes its appearance. The appellations 'East Sea' and 'Sea of Korea', or 'Sea of Japan', or to a lesser degree Sea of China will from this time on be present on almost all the published cartographic documents, from the map of Matteo Ricci until the modern maps.

Several Korean maps used the toponym 'Sea of Japan', and several Japanese maps used either 'Sea of Korea' or 'East Sea' from the map of Takahashi Kageyasu (1809), without forgetting

---

3) Note that from 1926 in the absence of Korea the toponym Sea of Japan was adopted by the International Hydrographic Office.
4) See Pelletier, "Tumulte of the Streams between Japan and Korea, about the Denomination of 'Sea of Japan'."

that map by Philipp Franz von Siebold as a European map, but one achieved with the help of Takahashi Kageyasu and other Japanese cartographers. There also are Ajia jido (1889), Oju Gakguk Tongsok Cheondo (1896), and the map of the world (1855) published by the Korean government.

Both parties rest their arguments in cartographic history. Japanese and European cartography followed international practices, and thus should prevail. For the Koreans, legitimacy is also found in indigenous naming practices, and the rehabilitation of the former name of this sea is the correction of an injustice committed against Korea. Both countries argue the merits of maps as a basis of their claim. But as noted above, not only do the maps not enjoy any credibility, but also desired in our case, both parties refer to maps produced by foreigners to justify their respective positions.We believe that our side uses the maps to justify a particular name. However, the shared space may not have shared that particular name and that particular name may not have been accepted by both.

Ⅴ. Policies of the UNGEGN Concerning the Denomination of Seas

If the Koreans and Japanese conducted an account of the different appellations of this sea to show the preeminence of one or another appellation, it appears that without going as far as counting all the maps and documents on which appears one or another appellation that a shared space can only have a shared appellation, with one name accepted by the oneside and another name by the otherside.

No appellation of a shared space that is not the subject of an agreement between the concerned parties can enjoy an exclusive use completely on the international level. It is in this perspective that several recommendations have been adopted by the different Conferences of the United Nations on the normalization of the geographical names, notably among them the sixth conference.

To briefly recall the goals and objectives of the UNGEGN, the group of experts has identified the following as goals:

a) to underline the importance of the normalization of geographical names at the national and international levels, and to demonstrate the advantages that may possibly ensue from this normalization;

b) to gather the results of work accomplished by national and international organs that deal with the normalization of geographical names and to facilitate the diffusion of these results to the Member states of the United Nations.

The UNGEGN also has four principles:

1) the group of experts acts as a consultative organ;

2) the decisions of the group of experts are submitted as recommendations in the Conferences of the United Nations on geographical names; if they are approved, they are submitted as one or several resolutions to the economic and social Council for definitive approval with the demand that the Member states assure them an advertisement and diffusion as widely as possible by such means and suitable circuits as professional organizations, scientific and research organs, and institutions of higher education.

The decisions of the group of experts have a nature of recommendations;

3) the group of experts does not address questions concerning national sovereignty;

4) in the practice of its functions the group of experts conform to the principles of the charter of the United Nations and to the disposition below: the international normalization of the geographical names must be founded on national normalization.

VI. Policies of the UNGEGN

By its recommendation III/20 on the normalization of the names of topographic details that spread beyond a single sovereignty, the sixth Conference of the United Nations on the normalization of geographical names recommends on the one hand that when the countries in which spread a same geographical detail give to this detail a different name, they endeavor to agree on a unique name for this detail, and on the other hand that when the countries in which spread a same geographical detail have different languages and do not succeed in agreeing on a single toponymic form, it is of general rule in international cartography that we accept the toponymic forms of each of the interested languages.

The practice consisting of adopting one only or some of the toponymic forms and excluding another systematically would not be justifiable nor appropriate. Only technical reasons could make it necessary, notably in the case of maps of small scale, to stop using toponymic forms corresponding to one or the other of the considered languages.

Other recommendations in relation to this topic have been adopted by the previous Conferences. (See annex 1.) At the last Conference, which was held in Berlin in August-September 2002, the report of the work of the Committee III underlines, after debate with regard to the problem of the appellation of this sea, as follows:

"The Committee encouraged the three countries to continue their efforts to find a solution acceptable to all taking into account relevant resolution, or else accepts to differ, and to report the outcome of their discussions to the next Conference. The chairman stated in his summary that individual countries cannot impose specific names on the international community and standardization can only be promoted when a consensus exists."

That is, this problem has always been the subject of debate within the Group of Experts of the United Nations charged with the normalization of geographical names.

Ⅶ. Conclusion:

"To name the things badly is to add to the misfortune of the world"
"Mal nommer les choses c'est ajouter au malheur du monde"

Albert Camus

"The conquering peoples imposed their own toponymic 'software' to the territory that they appropriated"

George P.

In conclusion it is noted

1) that this sea shared by several nations had at all times historically several appellations that were legitimate;

2) that these appellations have been used indifferently as well by the Koreans, the Chinese, and the Japanese without any distinction[5];

3) that no appellation imposed itself in an indisputable way on the international level;

4) that the antecedence of one toponym or another did not emerge in a distinct and indisputable way;

5) that on the international level the use of 'Sea of Japan', notably on the sea and ocean maps published by the International Hydrographic Office, imposed itself to the detriment of other appellations;

6) that in a logic of recuperation, of reconquest, of history restitution, the Korean authorities started a broad campaign of sensitization of the international community so that this sea would recover its former appellation;

7) that in good will, they proposed that this sea be named 'East Sea' instead of 'Sea of Korea';

---

5) See a Chinese map of 1530 and the Korean map Palto chongdo of 1481. See Pelletier, "Tumulte of the Streams between Japan and Korea, about the Denomination of 'Sea of Japan'."

8) and that the international community recommends an understanding between the peoples sharing this sea in order to find an appellation satisfactory for all, and also recommends the simultaneous use in international cartography of the two appellations 'Sea of Japan' and 'East Sea' in the meantime.

Brahim Atoui

Brahim Atoui is the Secretary General of the National Council for Geographic Information in Algeria. He acquired a doctoral degree from the University of Aix en Provence, France, and received a Ph.D. diploma from the University of Constantine in Algeria.

REFERENCES:

Chavannes, Edouard (1903), Two More Early Specimens of Chinese Cartography, *BEFO* 3. pp. 214-247.

Cortazzi, Hugh (1983), *Isles of Gold: Antique Maps of Japan*, Tokyo : Weatherhill.

Dahlgren, Erik (1911), *The Beginnings of Cartography of Japan*, Uppsala, K.W. Appelberg; Amsterdam, Meridian, 1977.

Lee, Ki-Suk (2002), *East Sea in World Maps*, Shinyou Printing Co.

Pelletier, Philippe (2000), Tumulte of the Streams between Japan and Korea, about the Denomination of 'Sea of Japan', *Annals of Geography* 613. pp. 279-305.

IHO Seeking Way to Resolve East Sea Name Dispute

Park Nohyoung

The naming dispute between Korea and Japan over the sea area between the Korean Peninsula and the Japanese Archipelago has been one of the hottest issues in the International Hydrographic Organization (IHO). The IHO is a rather modest organization in size, but a very specialized one. The IHO, like other international organizations, has been working on the basis of its own rules including its founding convention. However, it seems that the IHO and its Member States have not paid full attention on these rules which are relevant and to be applicable to the disputes including the one of 'East Sea' or 'Sea of Japan'. This article examines the legal status and main activities of the IHO. It will find what the IHO is obliged, recommended or advised to do and to what extent in particular for the geographical names by browsing the relevant documents of the IHO.

Ⅰ. Introduction

1. Brief history of the creation of the IHO: from the Bureau to the IHO

International cooperation in the field of hydrography began with a conference held in Washington, D.C. in 1899, followed by two others in St. Petersburg in 1908 and 1912. In 1919, 24 countries met in London for a hydrographic conference. A creation of a permanent body on hydrography was decided in that conference. The resulting International Hydrographic Bureau began its activity on June 21, 1921 with the participation of 19 Member States. At the invitation of H.S.H. Prince Albert I of Monaco, the Bureau was provided with headquarters in the Principality of Monaco. Korea under the Japanese colonial rule was not allowed to join the Bureau, and 'Sea of Japan' instead of 'East Sea' was listed in the first publication of the Special Publication 23 – Limits of Oceans and Seas. The Convention on the International Hydrographic Organization (hereinafter IHO Convention) was adopted on May 3, 1967 and entered into force in September 1970 by creating the IHO with its headquarters permanently established in Monaco.

2. Rationale for the IHO

National hydrographic offices provide services to assist the safe and efficient navigation of ships. The principal service is the provision of nautical information, including nautical charts, notices to mariners, sailing directions, data for integrated navigation systems and other products and services. The provision of accurate and up-to-date charts offers significant economic and commercial benefits through facilitation of maritime trade and other marine activities. It also helps to prevent accidents which may result in the loss of life and property and in pollution of the marine environment.

Because navigation is an international activity it is necessary to have a means of coordinating the work of national agencies and of standardizing products and services, in order to provide an effective world-wide service for mariners. The governmental parties to the IHO Convention desire to pursue their cooperation in hydrography on an intergovernmental basis.

3. Basic Instruments for the IHO

In addition to the IHO Convention, the General Regulations and Financial Regulations set forth the functioning of the IHO in detail. They are annexed to the IHO Convention, but they do not form an integral part thereof. General Regulations are intended to supplement the provisions of the IHO Convention. General Regulations were registered with the U.N. Secretariat along with the IHO Convention in 1970. Considering that treaties and international agreements are allowed to be registered with the U.N. Secretariat, it is interesting to see that the General Regulations, which are not an integral part of the IHO Convention, were so registered. The General Regulations along with the IHO Convention may be invoked by its Government Parties before any organ of the U.N. such as the United Nations Conference on Standardization of Geographical Names (UNCSGN).

Certain rules on technical and administrative activities of the IHO are found in resolutions adopted by the IHO. Thus, resolutions of the IHO are very important for the working of the IHO. However, there is no particular provision on the status of resolutions in the basic documents including the IHO Convention, although there are some provisions mentioning resolutions. For example, the Bureau must circulate to Members all reports, resolutions, recommendations and other documents of the Conference and its subsidiary bodies. Certain rules on resolutions are also found in relevant resolutions. First, all resolutions adopted by International Hydrographic Conferences must be compiled in one volume which is called the Repertory of Resolutions. Second, the amendments to existing resolutions or new resolutions may be proposed either by a Member State or the Bureau. Third, when a technical proposal is not accepted by Member States, it will be included in the Inactive Resolutions section of the Repertory of Technical Resolutions as a matter of record for future reference. Fourth, when the Bureau deals with technical or administrative questions by correspondence, in principle, a resolution may be adopted when it has received the required majority of votes in favor. If it does not obtain that majority, the question shall be closed and Member States informed of the fact.

Resolutions of international organizations such as the IHO are called institutional acts which govern their activities. Resolutions may be binding or nonbinding, and normative or procedural. There is no provision on the legal nature of resolutions in the IHO Convention. General principles of international law would apply to resolutions in the IHO with respect to their legal nature. For example, the legal consequences of these resolutions may depend on the substance and form of the resolution concerned. It seems that IHO resolutions are not normally binding in that they do not normally require Member Governments to do something but just suggest or recommend so. Resolutions adopted by the IHO may not be invoked before U.N. organs in the same way.

II. The Characteristics of the IHO

The IHO is an intergovernmental organization in that its members are the parties to the IHO Convention. There are 84 members as of August 2009.

The IHO must have 'a consultative and purely technical nature'. The IHO is a consultative agency. The activities of the IHO are of a scientific or technical nature, and must not include matters involving questions of international policy. Two of the four objects of the IHO reflect the consultative and technical nature of the IHO.

An object to bring about "the co-ordination of the activities of national hydrographic offices" is related to the IHO's consultative nature. Such a coordination would lead to a greater degree of standardization of charts and nautical documents and considerably improve the theory and practice of the science of hydrography. Another object to bring about "the greatest possible uniformity in nautical charts and documents" is related to the IHO's technical nature.

Here the meaning of the term 'technical' would clarify the nature of the IHO and its scope of activities. First, the literal meaning of the term 'technical' is "relating to the knowledge, machines or methods used in science and industry" and "relating to the knowledge and methods of a particular subject or job." Second, the term 'technical' may show a close relationship between science and technique as found from the common use of the term 'scientific-technical' elements. For example, Article 76 of the 1982 U.N. Convention on the Law of the Sea governs the extent of continental shelf. In order to establish the width and location of the continent-ocean transition zone (COT), this provision incorporates scientific-technical elements such as geological, geomorphological and geophysical ones. Third, the term 'technical' may show an opposing relationship between law and technique. In this respect, the term 'technical' may imply facts which are separated from law relating to obligations and rights. The activities of the IHO are not related to law but to facts. Thus, the activities of the IHO may not include questions of international 'policy' which may require value-judgment, which is separated from facts-finding.

Being a consultative agency, the IHO has no authority over the hydrographic offices of the parties to the IHO Convention. The IHO provides a forum for the improvement of services to marine navigation through the discussion and resolution of hydrographic issues at the international level, and assists Member Governments to deliver these services in the most cost effective way through their national hydrographic offices. On the other hand, the Bureau, the IHO's arm, must bring to the notice of the hydrographic or other competent offices of the Member Governments any hydrographic work of an international character and problems of general interest that it might be useful to study or to undertake. The Bureau must strive for the solution of such problems or the undertaking of such work by seeking the necessary collaboration between Member Governments. The Bureau, between sessions of the Conference, may consult the Member Governments by correspondence on questions concerning the technical functioning of the IHO. The Bureau is also expected to deal with matters which may not be dealt with directly between the Member Governments.

Ⅲ. Uniform Policy for Handling Geographical Names of the IHO

One of the objects of the IHO is to bring about "the greatest possible uniformity in nautical charts and documents." For this purpose, A4.1 Uniform Policy for Handling Geographical Names, a technical resolution, was adopted. In order to obtain approximate uniformity in the geographical names appearing on its charts and other nautical documents, each national Hydrographic Office of maritime countries is recommended to do the following. This resolution finds five occasions where approximate uniformity in the geographical names appearing on the nautical documents of maritime countries is obtained: i) on its charts and other nautical documents of its own coasts; ii) on its charts and other nautical documents of foreign coasts where the Roman alphabet is officially used by the sovereign country; iii) on its charts and other nautical documents of foreign coasts where the script of the sovereign country is other than the Roman alphabet; iv) on its charts and other nautical documents of all foreign coasts for the generic part of complex geographical names; and v) on all its charts and other nautical documents for international sea areas. Resolution A4.1 is solely based on the assumption that geographical names are for those coasts of sovereign countries.

First, with respect to its own coasts, each national Hydrographic Office is recommended to show names that are in exact agreement with the forms prescribed by the most authoritative source in the country concerned. The geographical name is provided in its own official script, whether Roman or non-Roman. Complete and authoritative name coverage is used by all other Hydrographic Offices for the same area. It is to be noted that there must be the forms prescribed by the most authoritative source in a country for geographical names to be shown on its charts and other documents of its own coasts. Without the forms prescribed by the most authoritative source in a country or such authoritative source there would be no complete and authoritative geographical name coverage to be used in that country.

Second, with respect to foreign coasts, each national Hydrographic Office, where the Roman alphabet is officially used by the sovereign country of foreign coasts, is recommended to show names that are in exact agreement with the most authoritative usage of the country having sovereignty. Those geographical names are advised to be obtained directly from new and revised editions of the nautical charts and other documents of the country having sovereignty or confirmed by correspondence with that country. It is to be noted that geographical names of foreign coasts of the sovereign country only are respected.

Third, with respect to foreign coasts, each national Hydrographic Office, where the script of the sovereign country is other than the Roman alphabet, is recommended to show names that are obtained by applying the various international systems for Romanization approved by the U.N. to the names appearing on the most authoritative sources of the country having sovereignty or confirmed by correspondence with that country. It is to be noted that geographical names of foreign coasts of the sovereign country only are respected.

Fourth, with respect to all foreign coasts for the generic part of complex geographical names, each national Hydrographic Office is recommended to use the word (in its Roman-alphabet form) used by the country having sovereignty. By following this practice, the geographical generic term will not be translated but will appear, in its Roman-alphabet form, on the charts of all nations.

Fifth, with respect to names of countries, major territorial divisions and boundary features, and to the oceans and international subdivisions thereof, each national Hydrographic Office is recommended to apply its conventional national usage to them. Thus, it may show geographical names of the oceans and their international subdivisions by applying its conventional national usage. If there are internationally used names for the same area, each national Hydrographic Office may also show them but in a subordinate manner. Thus the geographical names of those international sea areas may be shown in accordance with its conventional national usage or in accordance with both its conventional national usage and international usage. This system of handling geographical names will be applied until an international convention by the U.N. on standardization of internationally recognized names has been adopted.

IV. International Standardization of Geographical Names in the IHO

One of the objects of the IHO is to bring about "the greatest possible uniformity in nautical charts and documents." For this purpose the IHO has been involved with international standardization of geographical names on its own and in cooperation with other relevant organizations. First, the Bureau is recommended to co-operate with the United Nations Group of Experts on Geographical Names (UNGEGN) with the object of achieving international standardization of names of maritime and undersea features. Second, the Bureau is also recommended to co-operate with the United Nations Group of Experts in the study of existing national and international practices concerning the delineation and naming of oceans and seas, including their integral subdivisions, beyond the limits of national jurisdiction, with a view to recommending improvements in current nomenclatural practices and procedures. It is to be noted that international practices concerning the naming of oceans and seas, including their integral subdivisions, beyond the limits of national jurisdiction, are not fixed but to be improved. Thus, the Bureau, after the cooperation with the UNGEGN, is asked to recommend improvements in current nomenclatural practices and procedures. Third, there might be a case where two or more countries share a given geographical feature such as, for example, a bay, strait, channel or archipelago under a different name form. In this case, the following set of processes is recommended for those countries.

In the first place, they are asked to endeavor to reach agreement on fixing a single name for the feature concerned. Thus, they may have to enter into negotiations for agreeing to a single name. In the second place where they have different official languages and cannot agree on a common name form, the name forms of each of the languages in question are recommended to be accepted for charts and publications unless technical reasons prevent this practice on small scale charts. Thus, they may have to accept the name forms of each of the languages in question for charts and publications if this practice is not prevented on small scale charts for technical reasons as with English Channel/La Manche.

V. Relevance of the IHO for the Naming Dispute over East Sea

Korea was not allowed to participate in the establishment of the IHO from the beginning, and thus it could not contribute to its activities including the publication of S-23 which lists only 'Sea of Japan'. As shown above, the principles over handling geographical names in the IHO have been developed over sovereign countries. Thus, Korea had no voice in the IHO while it was under Japanese colonial rule.

The IHO has adopted many resolutions, and one of them deals with international standardization of geographical names. The IHO asks the Member States in dispute to agree to a single name, and, if it is not possible, the name forms of each of the languages in question are recommended to be accepted. Thus, as long as there is no agreement between Korea and Japan, then 'East Sea' should be accepted along with 'Sea of Japan'. The IHO and its Member States should observe these principles reflected in its own resolution. If these principles are found inadequate, then they should be improved in the IHO.

Park Nohyoung

Park Nohyoung is a professor of international law at the Law School of Korea University in Seoul, Korea. He holds a doctorate from University of Cambridge, an LL.M. from Harvard Law School, and an LL.B. from Korea University. His area of specialization covers international economic law such as the WTO law, and dispute resolution, such as negotiation and mediation. He recently served as commissioner of the Korea Trade Commission (comparable to the USITC), and chair of the Geographical Indication Registration Committee in Korea. He is currently president of the Society for East Sea.

Possible Solutions

The sea of the Three Endonyms: How Maritime Names like "East Sea" or "Sea of Japan" Fit into Two Categories
Paul Woodman

"Donghae" and "Nihonkai": Impossible to Coexist?
Choo Sungjae

One Sea, Two Names: The Case of the "East Sea"
Shin Gil-sou

The Sea of the Three Endonyms: How Maritime Names like "East Sea" or "Sea of Japan" Fit into Two Categories [1]

Paul Woodman

Sometimes we concentrate so intently and at such length on a particular feature that we begin to lose sight of its true nature, and maybe that has been the case with the maritime feature that we know in the English language as the 'East Sea' or the 'Sea of Japan.' Much of the material written about this sea – and its name – regards it as a political feature, or a diplomatic feature, or an economic feature, or a feature of substantial historical significance. Rarely does a paper or article convey the basic fact that, at heart, this is simply a geographical feature, an area of sea. This is its basic natural characteristic; all the other attributes are ones we have added in our minds as human beings.

For my part, I certainly find it helpful to look at this sea as a natural feature, and to do so in the context of the ongoing discussions taking place within the United Nations Group of Experts on Geographical Names (UNGEGN). One of the ways in which that forum distinguishes geographical names (also known as

---

1) This paper has been presented at *The 15th International Seminar on Sea Names* (2009).

toponyms) is by dividing them into the twin categories of endonym and exonym. As a quick and straightforward example of this distinction, the capital city of Austria is known locally in the German language as Wien, and so this is the endonym. The city is of course also named in languages not relevant to Austria, for example it is known in the English language as Vienna, and this type of name is an exonym.

How do maritime names such as the East Sea or Sea of Japan fit into these two categories? Let me first look at northeast England, since this is the area in which I grew up. As a child there, all the geographical names I used were in the English language and applied to features in the area where I lived, so those names fitted exactly the UNGEGN definition of an endonym, which is: Name of a geographical feature in an official or well-established language occurring in that area where the feature is situated.

As I played football on the beach at Tynemouth, there was land on one side of me and sea on the other. To me there was really no distinction between the two types of feature. The land which I called Northumberland, and the sea which I called the North Sea, were both equally integral parts of my local environment, both with English-language names, and looking back now with my UNGEGN experience I am certain that they are both endonyms.

When I looked out from Tynemouth over the North Sea, I knew that way beyond the horizon stood Denmark and Norway. And even though I could only see a tiny portion of this huge feature with my eyes, I never doubted that the entire sea was one single feature with one single name in my language. I could watch the ferry leaving the River Tyne for Denmark or Norway, and although it would soon disappear over the horizon I knew it would remain in this same geographical feature that I called the North Sea right up to the point at which it docked the following day. For me, from my perspective, my English-language endonym North Sea remained valid for the entire feature. And it was equally self-evident to me that a person living in Norway would name the same feature as Nordsjøen, its Norwegian language name, and would name it as such right up to the Northumberland coast where I was standing.

This perspective is, I believe, both instinctive and natural. It is also one that is entirely devoid of any questions of politics, exclusive economic zones, and suchlike. It is true that as I stood on the beach there were political differences between the land on one side and the sea on the other. The land is sovereign United Kingdom territory, whereas most of the sea is not. But that political question is a separate issue. The geographical feature to which I apply the toponymic label North Sea is one single feature right from the beach where I stood across to where the waves lap up on to the shore in Norway, Denmark, Germany, the Netherlands and Belgium. Calling this single feature by one single English-language name is simply the natural and logical thing to do, and does not in any way imply possession of the feature.

Now let us transfer our attention right round the globe and consider in a similar manner the sea that stretches between the Korean Peninsula and the Japanese archipelago. Is it really so different from the North Sea?

Let us imagine a Korean youngster watching the sunrise by the seashore in Gangwon Province. He too looks out eastwards on to a sea that stretches way beyond the horizon, all the way to Japan. And because he knows that this is all one and the same feature, he calls it by one name too: 'Donghae', or 'East Sea'. If he imagines a boat sailing eastwards out of the port of Gangneung towards Niigata in Japan, he will consider that the boat is crossing what he calls Donghae all the way to the point at which it docks at its Japanese destination. And there in Niigata itself, a Japanese teenager stands watching that same boat dock. It is evening, and looking westwards into the setting sun he thinks to himself that this boat has come from Korea and has crossed the entire width of the feature he knows as Nihon-kai, which translates into English as 'Sea of Japan'. Meanwhile, further north, that same sunset is being watched from the seashore of Primorskiy territory in Russia by a teenager who is admiring this evening view over the feature he knows as Yaponskoye More, which translates into English as 'Japanese Sea'.

All these youngsters, in South Korea, Japan and Russia, are using the endonym relevant to their own language for this single extensive maritime feature – just as I did in considering the North Sea from Tynemouth. And because one given name cannot be at the same time both an endonym and an exonym, so the conclusion must therefore be that this particular sea has in fact three endonyms – Donghae, Nihon-kai, Yaponskoye More – and that all three of these endonyms are applicable to the entire maritime feature. This sea can therefore truly be labeled as the 'Sea of the Three Endonyms'.

I believe we can easily reconcile this belief – that there are three endonyms for this sea – with our UNGEGN definition of 'endonym'. Let us look at this definition again: Name of a geographical feature in an official or well-established language occurring in that area where the feature is situated.

The definition requires firstly that there should be a geographical feature. Clearly that criterion is satisfied here; there is one single sea. The definition then asks that the names of that feature should be in official or well-established languages of the area concerned. Again, that criterion is satisfied since Japanese, Korean and Russian are all languages immediately relevant to this feature; they are all official and well-established along various sections of its shorelines. We should remember once more that the entire feature – not a portion or section of it – is the object that is named in these three languages. This too is in harmony with our definition; the relevant languages have to occur where the feature as a whole is situated, not where a certain portion of the feature is situated. So even though the three names are not all relevant to all shores they nevertheless constitute true endonyms.

Of course, it would be absurd to believe that in Japan the endonym Donghae has any local linguistic relevance, and it would be equally absurd to pretend that the endonym Nihon-kai has any local linguistic relevance in Korea. But if a Korean person is standing in Niigata and looking west out over the open sea, he will refer to that sea as Donghae and in doing so he will be using an endonym because he is using the Korean language, even though he is standing in Japan. Donghae is the Korean endonym for the feature in its entirety, right up to the point at which its waves lap against the pier at Niigata. Similarly, Nihon-kai is the Japanese endonym for the entire feature, right up to the harbour wall at Gangneung.

These toponyms are endonyms in their own local languages, in the forms 동해, 日本海, and Японское море, and also in the corresponding romanized forms. But the names for this sea in other languages, such as English, French and Spanish, are exonyms, because for those languages the criteria of the UNGEGN definition of an endonym are not satisfied. None of them – English, French, Spanish – occurs anywhere "in that area where the feature is situated." One consequence of this is that the English-language labels 'Sea of Japan' and 'East Sea' are both exonyms.

An atlas or map publisher faced with determining the correct name for such a feature therefore needs principally to consider the language of his target readership. If the publication is destined for a Korean readership, then 동해 (or Donghae) is the applicable name for the whole feature. If the publication is destined for a Japanese readership, then 日本海 (or Nihon-kai) is the applicable name for the whole feature. As we have seen, in both instances these publications will be using valid endonyms. For those language readerships further afield, such as English, French and Spanish, the name applied to this feature will be an exonym, and will be the traditionally used name in those languages for this feature.

Finally, it is important to note that this approach to the endonym really helps our discussions within the United Nations. Because it is genuinely legitimate to see even a large maritime feature as a single discrete whole, we are not placed in the invidious position of having to decide whether a particular toponymic label should stop at some (possibly disputed) sovereignty limit in the sea, and what other label should apply beyond that limit. Nor are we placed in the position of having to claim that a single maritime feature carries in the same language a name that is an endonym over one portion of its extent and an exonym over another; something which I consider to be impossible in logic.

In conclusion, I believe that the well-known political and diplomatic difficulties concerning the naming of this sea could be greatly assisted if we could start from the premise that we are dealing with what is first and foremost a straight forward geographical feature.

Paul Woodman

Paul Woodman spent his career of more than three decades at the Permanent Committee on Geographical Names (PCGN), an inter-departmental body which advises the U.K. government on the spelling of foreign geographical names. Thirty of those years (1979-2009) were spent as PCGN secretary, and from this position he sought to convey the cultural and political significance of geographical names in many forums, notably the UN Group of Experts on Geographical Names (UNGEGN), of which he has been a member since 1977.

'Donghae' and 'Nihonkai':
Impossible to Coexist?

Choo Sungjae

I. The 'Sea of Japan' in the Media

During my one-year stay in the United States from 2008 to 2009, I could often find news on Korea on broadcasting networks and in the newspapers. Such topics as the free trade agreement between Korea and the United States and the Korean people's candlelight demonstrations against it, the suicides of a famous actress and the former president and the missile launch by North Korea were among them. Some articles, mostly on North Korea's movements, were accompanied by a map showing the eastern part of Korea. All the maps, without exception, named the sea located to the east of Korea

Window on life in N. Korea closes

TOURS ACROSS BORDER
TENSE BUT REVEALING

Sign of deteriorating
relations with S. Korea

BY JEAN H. LEE
The Associated Press

KAESONG, North Korea — For months, tours of this historic city — famed for its Buddhist temples, royal tombs and ancient relics — have given South Koreans a glimpse of life in the hidden communist North.

But North Korea officials announced Monday that these visits were being suspended starting Dec. 1 because of tensions with Seoul — not that they were that truly welcoming anyway: On a weekend visit, cellphones, laptops and cameras with telephoto lenses were locked away even before the tour bus left South Korean territory.

more than 110,000 tourists have visited Kaesong, a city just 40 miles from Seoul but inaccessible for nearly 60 years.

North Korea's announcement Monday that the tours will be suspended has heightened fears that 10 years of progress in improving ties between the wartime rivals may

THE SEATTLE TIMES

<Figure 1> The Seattle Times,
11/25/2008, A7

as 'Sea of Japan'.

I wrote to the editor of a local newspaper, the Seattle Times, to inform that many map publishers, appreciating the name 'East Sea' as well as 'Sea of Japan', use both names in their maps and argued that in such a small-scale map centered on Korea, it would be more appropriate to use the name that Koreans use. I added that, by the same token, 'Sea of Japan' should be used on a map of Japan and that many commercial map makers adopt this way of balancing regarding this issue.

Unfortunately, I did not receive any reply to my comment, but it did not take long to find out from other sources that American newspapers have no other choice but to use standard names appearing in the United States Board on Geographic Names database. This shows the power of the standardized name for a geographical feature with designated limit. As the whole body of water between Korea and Japan is standardized as Sea of Japan, even the sea close to the Korean coast should be named as such.

II. People's Perception Reflected in the Geographical Names

Experts in the field of toponymy, the science of place names, emphasize that the geographical name that local people use in their own language should be given the highest priority in its standardization. This type of name is called 'endonym'. More precisely, endonym is defined as "name of a geographical feature in an official or well-established language occurring in that area where the feature is situated." According to this definition, 'Donghae' is an endonym of the sea located in the east of Korea because it is in Korean, the official language occurring in this area.

But the problem here is that to what limit of sea Korean is the official language. This is related to the issue of sea boundaries including territorial waters, the high sea and the exclusive economic zone. What I want to note, as a geographer, is people's perception of the sea limits. For example, to what limit of sea in the east of them would Korean people perceive as 'their' sea, Donghae? To what limit of sea in the west of them would Japanese people perceive as 'their' sea, Nihon-kai?

People's perception is important because it is reflected in naming their places. For example, Native Americans regarded themselves as a part of nature, not the master of it. This perception led them to have very descriptive place names, such as Mississippi (big river), Tacoma (mother of waters), Issaquah (sound of birds), etc. Even more, they had longer names such as "where there is heap of stones." This is similar to calling something "the house with red roof at the corner of the playground."

We need well-designed surveys to correctly answer the question of sea limits. But I suppose the ordinary people's perception, not the fishermen's nor the marine scientists', would be centered on the coastal areas, as the place of enjoying the beach and sea bath, fishing, or boating, where people have strong emotional ties. An old map made as early as 1530, titled Paldo-Chongdo meaning a general map of eight provinces, clearly shows this point. The name Donghae (東海) does not appear in the sea, but in the eastern coast where a religious service was given to the maritime god. This reflects the fact that people's perception of the sea at that time was centered on coastal waters.

It would not be easy to divide Koreans' Donghae and Japanese' Nihonkai based on perception and it would require further study on either side of Korea and Japan. But it seems quite certain that there would be very little overlap between these two segments. There must be very few Koreans who perceive the sea which is not visible from Dokdo, the far eastern island of Korea, as Donghae.

This implies that two exclusive names, which could be called as endonyms for each party, can coexist. But a critical problem happens when there is need to have one standardized name, either for a document or for a map. There could be a serious controversy surrounding this name. Many ill feelings are evoked by a map which writes 'their' name on the sea area we perceive as 'ours'.

Ⅲ. Geographical Feature, the Possibility of Giving Separate Names

A famous Israeli toponymist Prof. Naftali Kadmon, in his paper submitted to the U.N. in 2007, pointed out that covering territorial waters of Korea with the name 'Sea of Japan' would be problematic because this is the area where the Korean language is officially spoken by Korean people. He also argued that it would be appropriate to employ preferably both names for the area outside of the territorial waters. In this discussion, I believe, is implied the possibility of separating sea areas and naming each portion of them: one for territorial waters of A country, one for territorial waters of B country and one for the high sea between them.

We find a case of separating waters in the area between United Kingdom and France. The eastern end of the English Channel (La Manche) was separated as the Dover Strait (Pas de Calais) in 2002 by International Hydrographic Organization (IHO). This case of separation, in spite of there not being discernable recognizable identity, opens the possibility of separating sea areas on the basis of territorial limits.

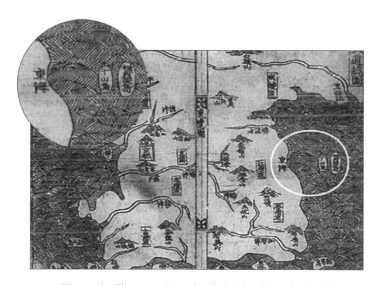

<Figure 2> The name *Donghae* in Paldo-Chongdo (1530)
(General Map of Eight Provinces)

Separation of geographical features and subsequent naming of each separated feature should be based on the perception of people who are embedded into the feature. Native Americans' perception of geographical features was confined to a part of river or mountain, not the whole feature. As the result, they did have place names for a bend or a rock, but did not have ones for the whole river or mountain.

If it is possible to separate the sea between Korea and Japan, then it would be much easier to argue that it should be called Donghae or 'East Sea', at least for the territorial waters of Korea. In small scale maps, where writing all these separated names is not possible, adopting dual names would be a viable solution.

Ⅳ. 'Donghae' or 'East Sea'?

Donghae is an endonym which has long been used by Koreans in their language. Why not use this original form instead of the translated one, 'East Sea'? I would argue that due respect should be given to the specificity of oriental languages. Such languages as Korean, Chinese and Japanese have completely different writing scripts and etymology from those using roman alphabets and it is therefore very difficult to convey the meaning of the names in the international use. The need for translation of names happens here.

A recent trend of simplifying Chinese transcribed names supports this argument. All the transcribed names in the former document of IHO, Tung Hai, Nan Hai and Hwang Hai for East China Sea, South China Sea and Yellow Sea, respectively, were deleted in a recent version.

The name 'East Sea' could be categorized as translated form of the endonym Donghae. This category deviates from the requirements of an endonym, which should be in an official or well-established language but becomes acceptable when we call it 'translated form'. Translated forms of Donghae other than English would include Ostmeer in German, Mer de l'Est in French, Mar del Este in Spanish and Восточное Море in Russian.

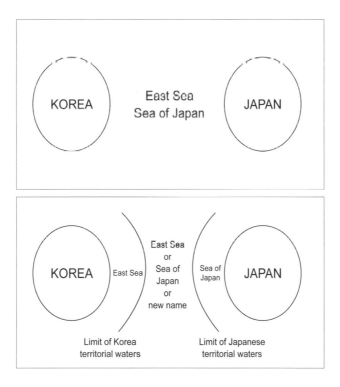

<Figure 3> Viable solution for the name between Korea and Japan(above for large-scale maps, below for small-scale map

Choo Sungjae

Choo Sungjae is professor of geography at Kyung Hee University in Seoul. He is currently vice president of the Society for East Sea. Choo earned his bachelor's and master's degrees in geography at Seoul National University and his doctoral degree at State University of New York at Buffalo.

One Sea, Two Names : The Case of the "East Sea"

Understanding on the naming dispute over the 'East Sea' / 'Sea of Japan' and the perspective of Korean government on the issue.

Shin Gil-sou

Historically, the sea area between the Korean Peninsula and the Japanese Archipelago has been called 'East Sea' in Korea for the past 2,000 years. Until the 19th century, maps published in Europe designated this area with various names such as 'Sea of C[K]orea', 'East Sea', 'Sea of Joscon', 'Sea of Japan', and 'Oriental Sea'.

However, this sea area became more widely known as the 'Sea of Japan' after the International Hydrographic Organization (IHO) chose to use the name 'Japan Sea' in its 1929 Special Publication *Limits of Oceans and Seas* (also called S-23). IHO was established in 1921 to support safety of navigation and the protection of the marine environment and published S-23 in 1928 in an effort to establish international limits and names of oceans and seas. In 1929, member states of the IHO approved the publication in which only the name 'Japan Sea' was used. It was this publication that largely led to the internationally wide use of 'Sea of Japan'.

Regrettably, Korea could not voice its objections at the time as it was under Japanese colonial rule. Korea was colonized by Japan in 1910, but even before that, Korea had already been deprived of its diplomatic representative by Japan in 1905. Korean people, with their nation under Japanese colonial rule, were forced to use the Japanese language for the designations of mountains and seas, and even their own names.

However, the Japanese government asserts that the name 'Sea of Japan' has no connection with Japan's colonial rule in the 20th century and the name was internationally established prior to the 19th century. Accordingly, Japan insists that only the name 'Sea of Japan' is usable, leaving no room for a solution acceptable for Korea and Japan.

While 'East Sea' is less known today due to historical circumstances of the late 19th and early 20th centuries, its legitimacy is firmly grounded in relevant IHO's resolutions on geographical names and general toponymic principles as well as historical documents and world maps.

Ⅰ. Toponymic Principles: The Name used by the Local People Should be Given the Highest Priority

Geographical names are an expression of perceptions of a place, a means of communication about the place and a way of referencing. Since geographical names are a part of the lives of the people who use them, it is common practice to give the highest priority to the names used by local people when deciding on a name for international use. It is also well provided in United Nations Conference on the Standardization of the Geographical Names (UNCSGN) resolution I/4 "Further recognizing that national standardization of geographical names by all nations is an essential preliminary to international standardization."

'East Sea' is the name that has been used by 75 million South and North Korean people for over 2,000 years. Its historical legitimacy is demonstrated by various documents and maps. In contrast, rather than creating the name 'Sea of Japan' for themselves first, the Japanese only adopted the name following its usage by the West.

II. Concurrent Naming before Agreement

As seen in the map, the sea body is shared by four countries — South Korea, North Korea, Russia and Japan. Within the sea area are the territorial waters and Exclusive Economic Zones (EEZ) of each

<Figure 1> A Map of 'East Sea'

country found. It is therefore not appropriate to name this sea body after one particular country when several countries share sovereignty and jurisdiction.

Relevant international organizations recommend that names be used concurrently when countries concerned cannot agree on a single name for a shared geographical feature. IHO Technical Resolution A.4.2.6 and the United Nations Resolution on the

---

IHO Technical Resolution A.4.2.6 (1974)

It is recommended that when two or more countries share a given geographical feature (such as, for example, a bay, channel or archipelago) under a different name form, they should endeavour to reach agreement on fixing a single name for the feature concerned. If they have different official languages and cannot agree on a common name form, it is recommended that the name form of each of the languages in question should be accepted for the charts and publications unless technical reasons prevent this practice on small scale charts e.g. English Channel/La Manche.

United Nations Resolution on the Standardization of Geographical Names III/20 (1977)

Names of features beyond a single sovereignty

"The Conference,

Considering the need for international standardization of names of geographical features that are under the sovereignty of more than one country or are divided among two or more countries,

1. Recommends that countries sharing a given geographical feature under different names should endeavor, as far as possible, to reach agreement on fixing a single name for the feature concerned ;

2. Further recommends that when countries sharing a given geographical feature do not succeed in agreeing on a common name, it should be a general rule of international cartography that the name used by each of the countries concerned will be accepted. A policy of accepting only one or some of such names while excluding the rest would be inconsistent in principle as well as inexpedient in practice. Only technical reasons may sometimes make it necessary, especially in the case of small-scale maps, to dispense with the use of certain names belonging to one language or another."as was proven in the editions of "Limits of Oceans and Seas: S-23" published so far.

Standardization of Geographic Names III/20 support Korea's perspective in favor of concurrent use of 'East Sea' / 'Sea of Japan'.

Reaching an agreement on a common name for a sea adjacent to several countries is obviously a difficult and sensitive task, since the name of the sea reflects the culture, history and identity of the people living nearby.

Therefore, the rational resolution to the naming dispute over the sea body between the Korean Peninsula and the Japanese Archipelago is the concurrent use of both name, 'East Sea' and 'Sea of Japan', until the two countries agree on a common designation, in accordance with the IHO Resolution and United Nations Resolution.

Since 2002, Korea has held five bilateral meetings with Japan in order to pursue constructive dialogue and reach an agreement on a common name. However, Japan has only responded with indifference to Korea's perspective and continues to insist that nothing other than the single use of 'Sea of Japan' is acceptable.

III. Old Maps with Dual Names for the 'East Sea' Area

Actually, the two names for the 'East Sea' area is not newly formulated idea. Even in the old maps are the several cases of two names in the sea body often found.

Robert de Vaugondy was a royal geographer and leading cartographer in France during the 1700s. Unlike other carto-

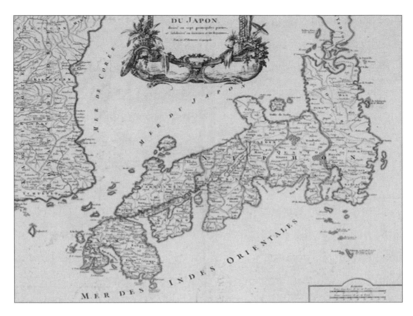

<Figure 2> L'Empre du Japon by Gilles Robert de Vaugondy (France, 1750)

graphers, he named the sea adjacent to the Korean Peninsular 'MER DE CORÉE,' and the sea adjacent to Japan 'MER DU JAPON'. Similar patterns of naming the 'East Sea' were also found in maps published by Robert Dudely in the 17th century and Jean-Baptiste Nolin in the early 18th century (fig. 2).

The original copy of this map (fig. 3) was made by a French royal geographer Guillaume Delisle, the most distinguished cartographer of his time, in 1723. Later in 1805 and 1819 the map was revised by Dezauche who was a geography professor as well as expert in cartographer with several years of professional career in Naval Institute of Cartography. The 'East Sea' area was named as 'MER DE CORÉE' in the original copy, but it has named as

<Figure 3> Carte D'Asie by Dezauche (France, 1819)

<Figure 4> Carte De L'Epire De La CHINE by E. Mentelle & P.G. Chanlaire (France, 1803)

'MER DE CORÉE ou du JAPON' since 1805.

This map (fig. 4) was created by E. Mentelle and P.G. Chanlaire.

Mentelle was formerly professor of geography and history at the Military School. This map is based on R. Bonne's map of China, Korea and Japan, but incorporates a lot of information from la

<Figure 5> Kankyo Dainibon Sizin Zenzu by Hashimoto Kyokuransai
(Japan, 1868)

Pérouse's map. This is evident from the use of names such as 'I. Dagelet' and 'Detroit de la Perouse' On 'East Sea', the inscriptions of 'MER DU JAPON' in the centre and 'Mer de Corée' to the Korean Peninsula are shown.

Map of Japan (fig. 5) and its adjacent region by Hashimoto Kyokuransai, a Japanese artist and cartographer. In this map produced with Japanese government permission, he placed 'Sea of Joseon'(朝鮮海) along with the east coast of the Korean peninsula

<Figure 6> Nieuwe Kaart Van't Keizerryk CHINA by I. Tirion (Dutch, 1740)

and 'West Sea of Japan'(日本西海) at the west coast of Japan.

This is a map(fig. 6) of China with place names in French and Dutch by I. Tirion. In 'East Sea', there are even three names accordingly to its adjacent geographical features. The southmost one, 'Mer Septentrionale du Japon' (faintly 'Noord Zee van Japan'), just north of that, 'Mer de Coree' and further north, 'Mer de Kamtzchatka'. Whether it is because of the lack of space, there is no name for the Pacific Ocean. The southern exit of East Sea is 'Detroit de Coree / Engte van Corea' and eastern exit is 'Detroit du Japon / Engte van Japan'.

IV. Recent International Notations

Recently, there were some notations from international organizations. In the 17th IHO Conference, held in Monaco, 2007, it was suggested that a revised version of the book *Limits of Oceans and Seas* (S-23) be published into two volumes, one including agreed issues and the other containing unresolved matters, like the dispute over 'East Sea' and 'Sea of Japan'. This suggestion could not be accepted because Japan showed opposing position to this.

In the 9th UN Conference on Geographical Names held in New York, 2007, the debates were repeated again and bilateral or trilateral talks were encouraged and the results of the talks should be reported in the next conference in 2012.

Ⅴ. The Name at Present

In fact, many of the world's prominent cartographers and the press are beginning to recognize the validity of the name 'East Sea', and have moved away from the single use of 'Sea of Japan' to the concurrent use of both names. In some cases they even use only the name 'East Sea'.

These demonstrate that the world has begun to recognize that the single use of 'Sea of Japan' is problematic. Such trends suggest growing support and understanding for the name 'East Sea' in the international community.

Japan is also starting to acknowledge that many map-producing companies are changing from the single use of 'Sea of Japan' to the concurrent use of 'East Sea' and 'Sea of Japan'.

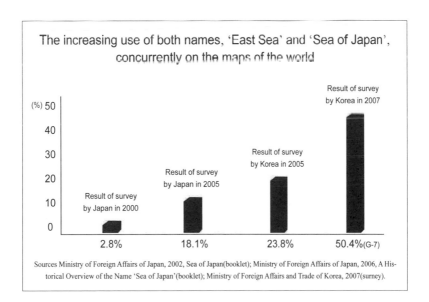

The increasing use of both names, 'East Sea' and 'Sea of Japan', concurrently on the maps of the world

Result of survey by Korea in 2007

(%) 50
40
30
20
10
0

Result of survey by Korea in 2005

Result of survey by Japan in 2005

Result of survey by Japan in 2000

2.8%   18.1%   23.8%   50.4%(G-7)

Sources Ministry of Foreign Affairs of Japan, 2002, Sea of Japan(booklet); Ministry of Foreign Affairs of Japan, 2006, A Historical Overview of the Name 'Sea of Japan'(booklet); Ministry of Foreign Affairs and Trade of Korea, 2007(surney).

Ⅵ. Its Position of Korean Government

Given the historical background of this sea area and the above mentioned international standardization rules, the exclusive use of the 'Sea of Japan' in the sea body cannot be justified under any circumstances. As a matter of fact, it is simply unnatural that our beautiful coast in the east should be called the 'Sea of Japan'. Furthermore, it is absurd that our offshore islands, Ulluengdo and Dokdo, should float on the surface of the 'Sea of Japan'.

Korea wishes to continue to engage in open discussions with Japan on the naming of the sea. Korea neither insists on the single use of 'East Sea' nor ignores the name 'Sea of Japan', which is used by 130 million Japanese people. Korea simply seeks Japan's respect and acknowledgement of the name which has been used for 2,000 years of Korean history and is still being used by 75 million South and North Korea.

The Korean government therefore calls upon the international community to use both names, 'East Sea' and 'Sea of Japan', until an agreement is reached on a name acceptable to both parties through bilateral consultations.

With a number of sensitive historical and political issues facing the two countries, the agreement on concurrent use of both names must serve as a catalyzing dynamics for Korea and Japan to create more harmonious and cooperative relationships in the future.

Shin Gil-sou

Shin Gil-sou is currently the ambassador for the Doha Development Agenda negotiations under the World Trade Organization. He previously served as ambassador at-large for Geographic Naming at the Northeast Asian History Foundation. Other previous positions include ambassador to the ICAO and Consul General in Montreal, minister for the Republic of Korea embassy in Manila and deputy director-general for multilateral trade negotiations of Seoul's Ministry of Foreign Affairs and Trade. With a bachelor's degree in economics from Seoul National University, he began his career as a public servant in 1978.

Interviews

Korea Pushes for Neutral Name for "Sea of Japan"

Lee Ki-suk

"Scholar sees possibility of Japan willing to find peaceful solution to dispute."

If one were to have asked Lee Ki-suk, a geographer and professor emeritus of Seoul National University, about the prospects of the controversial 'Sea of Japan' name being replaced with 'East Sea' 10 years ago, he may have replied: 'next to hopeless'.

His resentment over this sticky issue rings throughout his paper, titled "The Historical Precedent for the Geographical Name of 'East Sea (Sea of Japan)'," published in the *Virginia Geographer* in 1999.

In the conclusion, Lee says: "My government followed the U.N. (United Nations) suggestion and IHO (International Hydrographic Organization) resolution, and sought to engage Japan in a constructive dialogue to find a mutually acceptable solution. However, no progress has been made, because Japan refuses to enter into serious discussion. This attitude unfortunately appears unlikely to change in the foreseeable future."

Today, however, his skepticism has changed to optimism, with the rainbow of hope glaring in his path.

"The South Korean government has been making great efforts since 1991 to present our case to the U.N. and since 1997 to the IHO, and thanks to our tenacity, the issue is being addressed by some IHO member countries through a working group formed in June 2009," Lee told The Korea Herald. "This means Japan has acknowledged that there is an issue and has realized that it is difficult to ignore. I interpret this as Japan having the will to find a peaceful resolution."

He noted that over 20 nations are interested in the issue. Some of them, including South Korea and Japan, are the United States, France, China, North Korea, Australia and Italy.

Lee explained that the IHO has sought proposals for a resolution from these interested countries.

The IHO is "an intergovernmental consultative and technical organization that was established in 1921 to support safety and navigation and the protection of the marine environment," according to its website. It states that one of its objectives is to "bring about the greatest possible uniformity in nautical charts and documents."

"The working group members are now in the middle of submitting proposals," Lee said.

The 'East Sea' and 'Sea of Japan' name controversy is part of the working group that is also discussing how to republish the 'Limits of Oceans & Seas', which is like a reference book of geographical maritime names for cartographers, Lee said.

Many regions consider this 3rd edition, originally published in 1953, out of date. Consequently, an updated draft edition was produced in 2002 but has yet to be ratified or published.

The body of water, called an 'Asian Mediterranean', according to Lee, commands an area spanning over one million square kilometers. The total area is about one-ninth of the United States and five times the Korean Peninsula.

Lee's 1999 research paper says that the total coastline of this sea body makes up more than 6,000 kilometers. It notes that about 36 percent belongs to the Japanese, 16.4 percent to Korea, and the rest to Russia. The sea traditionally served as a fishing ground for the neighboring countries, and was especially noted as a place for catching whales.

But Lee stresses that the sea's importance of location has been increasing in terms of the development of deep sea natural resources, sharing of the Exclusive Economic Zone, ecological deterioration due to the dumping of nuclear wastes, airspace sharing, and military strategic space.

South Korea argues that a neutral name - 'East Sea' - would be legitimate, as it would not be named after one single country. Using 'East Sea' is also not a new phenomenon. Korean historical records show the name used in written documents before the birth of Christ. It is also used on old Chinese maps after the 12th century.

The official use of 'Sea of Japan', in place of 'East Sea', by Japan began in the 1870s. Following extensive exploration of this region by Western countries, Lee says, 'Sea of Japan' became the popular name. This was then adopted as the standardized version at the International Hydrographic Conference in 1929.

"This standardization by the IHO in 1929 was during Japan's colonial rule over the Korea Peninsula (from 1910 and 1945), so it was a unilateral decision and absent of Korea's say," Lee said.

South Korea officially raised issue at the UN Conference of Standardization of Geographical Names held in New York in 1992 and 1998.

The South Korean government has proposed as an interim measure – until the issue is resolved – to use both 'East Sea' and 'Sea of Japan' simultaneously in official documents, maps, and atlases, following the general rules of international cartography.

Lee said he was approached by the Korean government in 1992 to aid in the nation's 'East Sea' agenda. The 70-year-old recalls being nervous about the proposal.

"I was at first wary about the whole thing because I'm a geographer. Then I had the chance to look at some relevant research papers and I found that the issue also had some relations to my field," he said. "I got involved in 1994 in the campaign as the civilian representative."

According to the expert, the controversial body of water has taken on various names since the 16th century: Joseon Sea, Oriental Sea, Gulf of Korea, 'Sea of Korea', 'Sea of Japan', Manchuria Sea, China Sea, and Eastern Sea.

Lee is currently a member of the National Academy of Sciences and honorary president of the Society for 'East Sea'. He has also been serving as convener of The Working Group on Evaluation and Implementation, United Nations Group of Experts on

Geographical Names since 2000, a role he will maintain until 2012.

"Well, until this matter is officially settled, the South Korean government hopes that both the 'East Sea' and 'Sea of Japan' can be used simultaneously," Lee said. "If our proposal wins favor by the international community, this case can act as a precedent for solving other similar disputes and can be used as a case study in international forums."

By Yoo Soh-jung (sohjung@heraldm.com)

Lee Ki-suk

Lee Ki-suk is a professor emeritus of geography at Seoul National University and a member of the National Academy of Sciences in the Republic of Korea. He is honorary president of the Society for East Sea and former president of Korean Geographical Society.

World Interest in the "East Sea" Name Needed

Kim Jin Hyun

I. Dignitary says international awareness of sea name could lead to peaceful resolution

Generating global interest is key in seeing the controversial 'Sea of Japan' name replaced with 'East Sea', or at least having both names officially used, a leading Korean expert on the 'East Sea' name dispute said.

"We need to be allied with countries all over the world that have an interest in this sea name issue, and we especially need the support of the United Kingdom, Germany, Russia, the United States and France," said Kim Jin-hyun, the founding member and inaugural chairman of The Society for the East Sea.

The reason for singling out the five countries is that they have recognized experts and a strong background in maritime and geographical issues, said Kim, who is now acting as an advisor with The Society for the East Sea.

The Korean government has been making efforts to address the importance of changing the name of the 'Sea of Japan' to 'East

Sea', arguing that Japan unjustly renamed the sea body during its colonial rule of Korea (1910-1945).

"We had no say in the naming process; it was made unilaterally by Japan during its occupation of the Korean Peninsula," Kim lamented. "So, we've been proposing that the two names – 'East Sea' and 'Sea of Japan' – be used simultaneously until a final international agreement is reached."

The Society for the East Sea has been at the forefront of Korea's efforts to rename the controversial body of water since the country became United Nations member in 1991. The Society for the East Sea, a unique group of civilian experts representing the multiple realms of society, including academia, media, law and publishing, was officially formed in 1994. Kim at that time was eyed as the most suitable figure to lead the fledgling institution.

Since then, the body has been active in raising its case at four United Nations Conferences on the Standardization of Geographical Names, which were in 1995, 1998, 2002, and most recently in August this year. It has also participated in eight conferences of the United Nations Group of Experts on Geographical Names and two International Hydrographic Organization conferences.

The South Korean government believes 'East Sea' is a legitimate name because it would not be named after one single country. The name is not a new one. Korean historical records show 'Donghae (East Sea)' used in written documents before the birth of Christ. It is also used on old Chinese maps after the 12th century.

Ⅱ. Japan's stance is to wait for the IHO decision.

The official use of 'Sea of Japan', in place of 'East Sea', by Japan began in the 1870s. Following extensive exploration of this region by Western countries, experts say, 'Sea of Japan' became the popular name, influenced by Japan's economic and political clout in international affairs. 'Sea of Japan' was eventually adopted as the standardized version at the International Hydrographic Conference in 1929.

"We need the interest of individual countries, because it is at the national level, for instance, that geography-related textbooks are published and the media outlets report and shape information," Kim said. "The influence on the IHO decision would be huge if the geography textbooks and news media of individual countries adopt the practice of using both the 'East Sea' and 'Sea of Japan'," stressed the distinguished figure who once served as government minister of science and technology.

The annual International Seminar on Sea Names, launched by The Society for the East Sea, has so far taken place 16 times. With research funding provided by the Korean government, the seminar has attracted the interest of about 245 scholars from 26 countries, and resulted in the presentation of 198 papers.

"Our country is the only one in the world to hold such a global seminar on sea names," Kim said.

The official, who is concurrently now serving as the chairman of the World Peace Forum, added: "If big media firms like the New York Times, the Financial Times, CNN, BBC and AFP make wide simultaneous use of both 'East Sea' and 'Sea of Japan', we would have a firm ground to stand on to seek an official request from the government of the respective countries to change the naming practice."

So far, various publications have adopted the dual naming system. Publications like 'Time Magazine' and 'National Geographic' have already begun to simultaneously use 'East Sea' and 'Sea of Japan'. Kim cited Turkey as another supporter of the dual naming practice.

"We've made big strides, but should big media firms of major economies like the United States, France and Russia begin the practice of using both names, this could trigger a global wave, and such achievement would also make it easier for us to persuade other media outlets to do the same," the 74-year-old said.

At the 16th International Seminar on Sea Names held on Aug. 20, 2010 in the Netherlands, Kim in his presentation stated: "The 'East Sea' naming problem is more than territorial and sovereign matters to Korea. It has to do with universal and fundamental values of openness, democracy, human rights, diversity and peace."

During this interview with The Korea Herald, the renowned figure with comprehensive experience ranging from a bureaucrat to entrepreneur expressed optimism about the controversy.

"I'm hopeful about the whole thing; I'm not sure about the timing, but if we persevere, I believe the public masses of various countries will eventually show their support of using both names," Kim said.

The public figure, who began his colorful and distinguished

career path as a journalist at the Dong-A Ilbo newspaper in 1957, explained that if a resolution, or 'peak', is 40 kilometers up, the distance traveled up until now could be seen as 10 kilometers.

"The UN's view is that this issue could officially be approached and solved at the inter-governmental foreign affairs level, as opposed to the current civilian level, if the dual naming practice is widely applied by the citizens of the country," Kim said.

By Yoo Soh-jung (sohjung@heraldm.com)

Kim Jin Hyun

Kim Jin Hyun is chairman of the World Peace Forum and chairman of the Committee for the Establishment of the National Museum of Contemporary History. He started his professional career as a journalist at Dong-a Ilbo and was promoted to editor-in-chief of the daily newspaper in 1984. Later he was appointed as the Minister of Science & Technology of Korea (1990-1993), President of the University of Seoul (previously Seoul City University) (1995-1999). He also served as chairman of the Board of the Korea Institute of Science & Technology Evaluation and Planning (1998-2007).

Appendix

Resolutions of the International Hydrographic Organization

Resolutions of the United Nations Conferences on the Standardization of Geographical Names

(※ Listed by Subject)

Resolutions of the International Hydrographic Organization

1.-   With the purpose of obtaining approximate uniformity in the geographical names appearing on the nautical documents of maritime countries, it is recommended that each national Hydrographic Office:

a)   On its charts and other nautical documents of its own coasts, show names that are in exact agreement with the forms prescribed by the most authoritative source. Each country will thus provide complete and authoritative name coverage in its own official script, whether Roman or non-Roman, for the use of all other national Hydrographic Offices that issue charts on various scales, and other nautical documents, for the same area.

b)   On its charts and other nautical documents of foreign coasts where the Roman alphabet is officially used by the sovereign country, show names that are in exact agreement with the most authoritative usage of the country having sovereignty. These names should be obtained directly from new and revised editions of the nautical charts and other documents of the country having sovereignty or confirmed by correspondence with that country. Where such names as officially written use accents or diacritical signs, these should be retained, even, and indeed particularly, when names are printed in capital letters.

c) On its charts and other nautical documents of foreign coasts where the script of the sovereign country is other than the Roman alphabet, show names that are obtained by applying the various international systems for romanization approved by the United Nations to the names appearing on the most authoritative sources of the country having sovereignty or confirmed by correspondence with that country.

Note: Among countries where the Roman alphabet is official, international uniformity in transcription systems would be advantageous to the various national governments. It is accordingly recommended that national Hydrographic Offices place before their governments the desirability of obtaining uniformity and urge the continuation of efforts for effective agreements through the United Nations. (see also C1.2).

d) On its charts and other nautical documents of all foreign coasts, use for the generic part of complex geographical names the word (in its Roman-alphabet form) used by the country having sovereignty. e.g. Falsterborev. By following this practice, the geographical generic term will not be translated but will appear, in its Roman-alphabet form, on the charts of all nations.

e) On all its charts and other nautical documents, apply its conventional national usage to names of countries, major territorial divisions and boundary features, and to the oceans and international subdivisions thereof. The names used internationally may also be show n but in a subordinate manner. This system will be applied until an international convention by the United Nations on standardization of internationally recognized names has been adopted.

A4.2   International Standardization of Geographical Names

1.-   It is resolved that the IHB should maintain continuous contact with the United Nations Organization and specifically with the United Nations Group of Experts on Geographical Names, for all studies or actions relating to geographical names involving or affecting hydrographic publications. The Bureau should insure that actions previously taken on hydrographic matters, with respect to names, within the IHO are brought to the attention of appropriate United Nations Conferences or working groups. The Bureau should also promulgate to Member States information on all significant developments on this subject as they occur.

2.-   It is recommended that, since national standardization of geographical names is an essential preliminary to international standardization, Hydrographic Offices encourage and support the establishment of national names authorities, following the principles and procedures recommended by the resolutions on this subject adopted by the United Nations Conferences on Geographical Names.

3.-   It is recommended that the IHB co-operate with the United Nations Group of Experts on Geographical Names with the object of achieving international standardization of names of maritime and undersea features.

4.-   It is further recommended that co-operation should, in particular, be extended in the undermentioned activities of the United Nations Group of Experts:

a) Study of existing national and international practices concerning the delineation and naming of oceans and seas, including their integral subdivisions, beyond the limits of national jurisdiction, with a view to recommending improvements in current nomenclatural practices and procedures.

b) Drawing up a system for naming undersea features beyond a single sovereignty and proposing it as a basis for preparing an international convention on the subject.

c)   Standardizing the definitions of undersea feature "terms and definitions" in order to promote their acceptance and use by names authorities.

d)   Developing procedures for international standardization of naming new undersea features as they are discovered, defined and identified in the future.

5.-   It is recommended that when Hydrographic Offices produce gazetteers or geographical dictionaries, these publications be standardized as far as possible in accordance with resolutions on the subject adopted by the United Nations.

6.-   It is recommended that where two or more countries share a given geographical feature (such as, for example, a bay, strait, channel or archipelago) under a different name form, they should endeavour to reach agreement on fixing a single name for the feature concerned. If they have different official languages and cannot agree on a common name form, it is recommended that the name forms of each of the languages in question should be accepted for charts and publications unless technical reasons prevent this practice on small scale charts. e.g. English Channel/La Manche.

A4.3   Naming of Undersea Features

1.-   It is agreed that Member States should strongly encourage marine scientists and other persons in their country wishing to name undersea features to:

a)   check their proposals with published Gazetteers of Undersea Feature Names, including the IHO/IOC publication B-8, "Gazetteer of Geographical Names of Undersea Features" shown (or which might be added) on the GEBCO and on the IHO small scale International Chart Series and its supplements of Geographical Names included on larger scale Regional International Bathymetric Chart

Series;

b) take into account the guidelines contained in the IHO/ IOC publication B-6 "Standardization of Undersea Feature Names", including the use of the Undersea Feature Name Proposal Form contained therein;

c) submit all proposed new names for clearance either to their appropriate national authority or, where no such national authority exists, to the IHB or IOC for consideration by the GEBCO Sub-Committee on Undersea Feature Names, which may advise on any potential confusing duplication of names.

2.- It is agreed that Member States invite publishers of ocean maps and editors of scientific journals in their country to require compilers and authors to provide written evidence of such clearance before accepting for publication any maps or scientific articles containing new names for undersea features.

Resolutions of the United Nations Conferences on the Standardization of Geographical Names (※ Listed by Subject)

1. UN Conferences on the Standardization of Geographical Names

I/2   Second United Nations Conference on the Standardization of Geographical Names

The Conference,

Noting the importance of the standardization of geographical names and the great interest shown in this subject by the numerous participants in the Conference from the States Members of the United Nations and members of the specialized agencies, as well as interested international organizations,

Appreciating the work that has been accomplished by the participants in this Conference, Recognizing the necessity of standardizing geographical names for both national and international usage,

Recommends to the Economic and Social Council that the second United Nations Conference on the Standardization of Geographical Names be held not later than the last quarter of 1970.

II/1 Third United Nations Conference on the Standardization of Geographical Names

The Conference,

Noting the results of the work accomplished in the standardization of geographical names by the States Members of the United Nations and members of the specialized agencies as well as by the interested international organizations,

Further noting that these results were for the greater part due to the impetus given by the First United Nations Conference on the Standardization of Geographical Names,

Recognizing the important contributions to this work made by the Second Conference, as reflected in the resolutions that have been adopted,

Further recognizing the necessity of continuing this important work,

Recommends to the Economic and Social Council that a third United Nations conference on the standardization of geographical names be held not later than the first half of 1977.

III/1 Fourth United Nations Conference on the Standardization of Geographical Names

The Conference,

Noting the importance and necessity of continuing the work on the standardization of geographical names on both the national and international levels by States Members of the United Nations,

Further noting the important contributions of this Conference, as well as the contributions of the First and Second United Nations Conferences on the Standardization of Geographical Names,

1.   Expresses its appreciation to the Government of Iran for its offer to act as host country for the fourth United Nations conference

on the standardization of geographical names;

2. Recommends to the Economic and Social Council that the fourth United Nations conference on the standardization of geographical names be convened in Iran not later than the first half of 1982.

III/24 Use of the Arabic language as a working language at future United Nations Conferences on the Standardization of Geographical Names

The Conference,

Considering that since 1975 the Arabic language has been a working language of the General Assembly of the United Nations and of some of its organs,

Noting that seven Arab States have participated in the Third United Nations Conference on the Standardization of Geographical Names and that not less than 15 such States are expected to participate in the fourth conference,

Noting also that the Arabic language is understood by eight delegations (other than those of Islamic States) attending the Third Conference and that the number of delegations that understand the language thus constitutes almost one third of the participating delegations,

Considering that the Arab States are willing to bear in part or in full the cost of making the Arabic language a working language of the fourth conference,

Recommends that Arabic be made one of the working languages of future United Nations conferences on the standardization of geographical names and meetings of the Group of Experts.

IV/1 Fifth United Nations Conference on the Standardization of Geographical Names

The Conference,

Noting the results of the work accomplished in the standardization of geographical names on both the national and international levels by the States Members of the United Nations,

Further noting the important contributions made by the Conference to this work,

Recognizing the necessity of continuing this important work,

1.   Expresses its appreciation to the Government of Canada for its offer to act as host for the Fifth United Nations Conference on the Standardization of Geographical Names;

2.   Recommends to the Economic and Social Council that a Fifth United Nations Conference on the Standardization of Geographical Names be held in Canada not later than the second half of 1987.

V/1 Sixth United Nations Conference on the Standardization of Geographical Names

The Conference,

Noting the positive results of the work accomplished on the standardization of geographical names at both the national and international levels by States Members of the United Nations,

Noting also the essential role played by the present Conference in the co-ordination of those efforts,

Recognizing the necessity of continuing this important work,

1.   Expresses its appreciation to the Government of Morocco for its offer to act as host for the Sixth United Nations Conference on the

Standardization of Geographical Names;

2.   Recommends to the Economic and Social Council that the Sixth United Nations Conference on the Standardization of Geographical Names be convened in Morocco in the second half of 1992.

V/7   National reports

The Conference,

Recognizing that the national reports submitted by each country to the United Nations conferences on the standardization of geographical names contain much information that is useful for the consideration of the various items of the agenda of the conferences,

Bearing in mind that, in order to make an adequate evaluation of the progress made by all participating countries, it is important that the documents relating to each item of the agenda be made available to the conferences on time and, when necessary, by each participating country,

1.   Recommends that the United Nations Secretariat, when sending invitations to Member States to participate in the conferences, attach a detailed plan (model) for the drafting of national reports, providing specific guidelines for countries to follow in reporting on the progress made in the standardization of geographical names since the preceding conference;

2.   Also recommends that the necessary steps be taken to ensure that all the national reports to be discussed at a conference are distributed to participating countries at least one month before the conference is due to begin.

V/8   Reports of international organizations concerned with the standardization of geographical names

The Conference,

Recalling Economic and Social Council resolution 1314 (XLIV) of 31 May 1968, by which the Council requested the United Nations Group of Experts on Geographical Names, inter alia, to collect information issued by international organizations dealing with the standardization of geographical names,

Considering that, in order to avoid duplicating the work done by various international organizations on the standardization of geographical names, the Group deems it advisable that those organizations themselves develop standardization activities, in co-ordination with the Group,

Recommends that all officers responsible for maintaining liaison with those international organizations prepare written reports on the activities of the organizations for submission to each United Nations conference on the standardization of geographical names and each meeting of the Group and that, in the absence of such liaison officers, the Secretariat request the organizations themselves to provide such reports.

VI/6   Seventh United Nations Conference on the Standardization of Geographical Names

The Conference,

Noting the positive results of the work accomplished on the standardization of geographical names at both the national and international levels by States Members of the United Nations,

Noting also the essential role played by the present Conference in the coordination of those efforts,

Recognizing the necessity of continuing this important work;

1.   Expresses its appreciation to the Government of the Islamic Republic of Iran for its offer to act as host for the Seventh United Nations Conference on the Standardization of Geographical Names;

2.   Recommends to the Economic and Social Council that the Seventh United Nations Conference on the Standardization of Geographical

Names be convened in the Islamic Republic of Iran in the second half of 1997.

VII/2   Eighth United Nations Conference on the Standardization of Geographical Names and twentieth session of the United Nations Group of Experts on Geographical Names

The Conference,

Noting the positive results of the work accomplished on the standardization of geographical names at both the national and international levels by States Members of the United Nations,

Noting also the essential role played by the present Conference and by the United Nations Group of Experts on Geographical Names at its nineteenth session,

Recognizing the necessity of continuing this important work,

1.   Recommends to the Economic and Social Council that the Eighth Conference on the Standardization of Geographical Names be convened in the second half of 2002;

2.   Also recommends to the Economic and Social Council that the twentieth session of the United Nations Group of Experts on Geographical Names be convened during the fourth quarter of 1999;

3.   Further recommends that the Economic and Social Council continue to support the important work of the secretariat of the Group of Experts regarding the standardization of geographical names.

VIII/16 Ninth United Nations Conference on the Standardization of Geographical Names and the twenty-second session of the United Nations Group of Experts on Geographical Names

The Conference,

Noting the progress made in the work of the standardization of geographical names, at both the national and international levels, by States Members of the United Nations,

Noting also the essential role played therein by the present United Nations Conference on the Standardization of Geographical Names and by the sessions of the United Nations Group of Experts on Geographical Names,

Recognizing the necessity of continuing this important work,

1.   Recommends to the Economic and Social Council that the Ninth Conference on the Standardization of Geographical Names be convened in the second half of 2007;

2.   Also recommends to the Economic and Social Council that the twenty-second session of the United Nations Group of Experts on Geographical Names be convened in 2004.

IX/1   Tenth United Nations Conference on the Standardization of Geographical Names and the twenty-fifth session of the United Nations Group of Experts on Geographical Names

The Conference,

Noting the achievements and the progress made in the work of geographical names standardization at both the national and international levels,

Noting also the essential role played by the present Conference and by the United Nations Group of Experts on Geographical Names at its twenty-fourth session,

Recognizing the necessity of continuing this important work with the support of the Economic and Social Council,

1.   Recommends to the Economic and Social Council that the Tenth United Nations Conference on the Standardization of Geographical

Names be convened in 2012;

2. Also recommends to the Council that the twenty-fifth session of the United Nations Group of Experts on Geographical Names be convened in the first half of 2009.

2. International Co-Operation in the Standardization of Geographical Names

II/31 A common understanding of the aims and objects of the international standardization of geographical names

The Conference,

Recognizing the desirability of attaining a common understanding of the aims and objects of the international standardization of geographical names,

1. Recommends the following general definition in connexion with the continuing study by the Group of Experts of the field of application of international standardization: "International standardization of geographical names is that activity aiming at the maximum possible uniformity in the form of every geographical name on the earth and of topographical names on other bodies of the solar system by means of national standardization and/or international agreement, including the achievement of equivalences between different writing systems";

2. Further recommends that, as far as possible, the standardized local names should be used in maps and charts which are intended for international use and also in all international publications in which geographical names do not appear in the running text, such as international time-tables or tables of international statistics. Where geographical names appear in the running text in international publications in a given language, exonyms may be used, but in such cases it is desirable that the standardized local geographical names should

also appear in brackets. II/33 International co-operation in the standardization of geographical names The Conference, Having discussed the problem of the international standardization of geographical names and its field of application, Recognizing the difficulty of this problem and the necessity of establishing contact with interested international organizations, such as the Universal Postal Union and the International Telecommunication Union, Recommends that the United Nations Group of Experts on Geographical Names continue to study this problem in co - operation with such organizations.

IV/2   Acceleration of work on standardization of geographical names

The Conference,

Noting that, during the period since the First United Nations Conference on the Standardization of Geographical Names there has been a change in emphasis from the execution of large special projects to a more general need for development of land use and natural resources, land redistribution, conservation of the environment and the preservation of natural resources, all of which necessitates unambiguous reference in the naming of physical entities,

Noting further that international organizations, aid authorities, government departments, engineering and mining contractors, and agencies concerned with land use, water resources, agriculture, mineral exploration and development require detailed general planning documentation and that geographical names constitute a major element in such documentation and in the identification of administrative elements, land title and a wide range of other legal documents,

Recognizing that discrepancies occurring in geographical names on maps have been experienced by all concerned with such subjects and that this confusion is compounded by similar disparities in the names to be found in material and documents issued for purposes such as transportation and tourism, economic studies and telecommunications, and that variant names result inevitably in doubt and sometimes total confusion causing unnecessary expenditure of time and money,

Recognizing further the cultural and social importance of geographical names, Recommends that the standardization of geographical names should be accelerated by all possible means.

V/6 Promotion of national and international geographical names standardization programmes

The Conference,

Recognizing the importance of geographical names as significant elements of the cultural heritage of nations, and the economic advantage of standardizing national geographical names,

Recommends that State authorities be encouraged to provide appropriate support to standardization activities and that the standardization of geographical names be recognized as an important part of their programmes of international co-operation and technical assistance.

VI/8 Information from countries regarding changes in geographical names

The Conference,

Bearing in mind the political changes which have occurred in the world during recent years and which have a direct bearing on geographical names,

Recommends that wherever possible, every six months countries transmit information regarding changes in geographical names to the Secretary of the United Nations Group of Experts on Geographical Names in order to enable the Secretariat to disseminate that information through the UNGEGN Newsletter or any other relevant publication, at its convenience.

3. Maritime and Undersea Feature Names

II/22   Standardization of maritime nomenclature

The Conference,

Recognizing that the increased interest and activities of countries in the marine environment require an improvement in international nomenclatural standardization,

Recommends that the United Nations Group of Experts on Geographical Names study existing national and international practices concerning the delimitation and naming of oceans and seas, including their integral subdivisions, beyond the limits of national jurisdiction, with a view to recommending improvements in current nomenclatural practices and procedures.

II/23   Names of Antarctic and undersea features

The Conference,

Noting that the high degree of agreement on Antarctic names reached by the nations actively interested in that area has been achieved through informal co-operation, including the adoption of similar naming policies and the exchange of information supporting new name proposals and counter-proposals, if any,

Recognizing that these procedures come within the established framework of national standardization bodies, Considering that these procedures are also applicable to co-operation on the naming of undersea features,

1.   Recommends that the United Nations Group of Experts on Geographical Names work on a model statement or statements on the treatment of undersea feature names that can be suggested for adoption by interested countries;

2. Recommends further that the United Nations Group of Experts on Geographical Names develop model forms for proposing names of undersea features and Antarctic geographical entities for consideration by national names authorities, patterned after those used by the United States Board on Geographic Names and by similar organizations in other countries, and a form or forms for use by a national names authority in notifying any interested countries or institutions of its intention to name an undersea or Antarctic feature.

II/26 Standardization of names of undersea features beyond a single sovereignty

I

The Conference,

Recognizing the importance of the international standardization of names of undersea features beyond a single sovereignty,

Recognizing further the absence nowadays of a definite system and procedure for naming such features,

Recommends that the United Nations Group of Experts on Geographical Names, in co - operation with the appropriate national and international organizations and, in particular, with the International Hydrographic Organization, draw up a system for naming undersea features beyond a single sovereignty and propose it as a basis for preparing an international convention on the subject.

II

The Conference,

Noting that problems of terminology of undersea features inhibit international standardization of geographical names employing these terms,

Noting further the discussions on terminology of undersea features that are in progress among various countries and with the oceanography profession,

Recommends that the United Nations Group of Experts on Geographical Names, in co - operation with interested national names authorities and international organizations, attempt to standardize the definitions of undersea feature terms and definitions and to promote their acceptance and use by names authorities.

III/21　Maritime feature names

The Conference,

Having considered resolution 22 of the Second United Nations Conference on the Standardization of Geographical Names,

Noting that the International Hydrographic Organization has designated a technical committee to recommend improvements in procedures for naming oceans and seas and their integral subdivisions - referred to as maritime features - beyond the limits of national jurisdiction,

Recognizing the progress made by the International Hydrographic Organization in standardizing names of maritime features,

1.　　Expresses its appreciation to the International Hydrographic Association for its offer to assist in United Nations programmes related to maritime features;

2.　　Recommends that the United Nations Group of Experts on Geographical Names co-ordinate its programmes with those of the International Hydrographic Organization.

III/22   Undersea feature names

I

The Conference,

Recalling resolution 26 of the Second United Nations Conference on the Standardization of Geographical Names,

Considering the increased activity in ocean research and the need to develop names to identify a rapidly growing number of newly discovered undersea features,

Recognizing that such names are required for certain hydrographic publications and for bathymetric charts or related material used for research documentation,

Noting that a set of procedures developed by the United Nations would, if implemented by all Member States, lead to a desirable degree of uniformity in naming new features, while also establishing a mechanism for resolving conflicts over or duplication of names,

Realizing the interest of the International Hydrographic Organization and the Intergovernmental Oceanographic Commission in standardizing not only procedures for naming but also the names themselves,

Recommends that the principles and policies, as well as the name proposal form put before the Conference, be submitted to the International Hydrographic Organization for the purpose of developing an agreed statement to meet requirements for an internationally acceptable set of guidelines designed to ensure maximum standardization of undersea feature names.

II

The Conference,

Noting that national and international organizations may employ different terms and definitions for undersea features,

Realizing that the United Nations Group of Experts on Geographical Names has elaborated a list of terms and definitions that differ from those approved and submitted to the Conference by the International Hydrographic Organization,

Recommends that the Group of Experts, in collaboration with the International Hydrographic Organization, develop, for international use, a joint list of terms and definitions for undersea features.

IV/12   Maritime and undersea feature names

The Conference,

Noting that the Working Group on Undersea and Maritime Features of the United Nations Group of Experts on Geographical Names has completed its tasks in regard to undersea features, as called for by resolution 22 of the Third United Nations Conference on the Standardization of Geographical Names,

Observing that work in maritime features has not been finished, but should be further co-ordinated with similar work of the International Hydrographic Office, as recommended by the Third United Nations Conference on the Standardization of Geographical Names in its resolution 21,

1.   Recommends that the task of the Working Group should be limited to maritime features;

2.   Further recommends that the Group of Experts should identify a point of contact to carry out essential liaison and communications regarding names of undersea features proposed by national bodies.

4. Names of Features Beyond a Single Sovereignty

I/8   Treatment of names of features beyond a single sovereignty

A.   GENERAL

The Conference,

Recognizing that some features common to, or extending across the frontiers of, two or more nations have more than one name applied to them,

Further recognizing that the names of some features of this kind have different applications or extent,

1.   Considers that it is preferable that a common name or a common application be established, wherever practicable, in the interest of international standardization;

2.   Recommends that the geographical names authorities of the nations concerned attempt to reach agreement on these conflicting names or applications.

B.   MARITIME AND UNDERSEA FEATURES

The Conference,

Having discussed some of the problems arising from a lack of international standardization of names of maritime and undersea features,

Recognizing the necessity for international standardization of names in and under ocean areas to promote the safety of navigation and to facilitate the exchange of scientific oceanographic data,

Noting that valuable initial steps have been taken towards standardization of both the nomenclature of hydrographic and undersea features and the geographical names of some of these features by the Intergovernmental Oceanographic Commission (IOC), the International

Hydrographic Bureau (IHB), the International Association of Physical Oceanography (IAPO), and member nations,

1.   Recommends that the proposed United Nations Permanent Committee of Experts on Geographical Names should:

(a)   Obtain from the Intergovernmental Oceanographic Commission (IOC), the International Hydrographic Bureau (IHB) and the International Association of Physical Oceanography (IAPO), full particulars of the work already accomplished by those organizations;

(b)   Establish means for the collection, approval and distribution by the United Nations of both a list of agreed terms and definitions for nomenclature of maritime and undersea features and an initial list of recommended geographical names for features requiring names;

(c)   Develop procedures for international standardization of naming new undersea features as they are discovered, defined and identified in the future; (d) Continue to consult with and, as appropriate, to use the facilities of IOC, IHB, IAPO and other relevant bodies to further United Nations objectives in international standardization of names of maritime and undersea features;

2.   Further recommends that copies of this resolution be forwarded immediately to IOC, IHB and IAPO.

II/23   Names of Antarctic and undersea features

The Conference,

Noting that the high degree of agreement on Antarctic names reached by the nations actively interested in that area has been achieved through informal co-operation, including the adoption of similar naming policies and the exchange of information supporting new name proposals and counter - proposals, if any,

Recognizing that these procedures come within the established framework of national standardization bodies,

Considering that these procedures are also applicable to co-operation on the naming of undersea features,

1.   Recommends that the United Nations Group of Experts on Geographical Names work on a model statement or statements on the treatment of undersea feature names that can be suggested for adoption by interested countries;

2.   Recommends further that the United Nations Group of Experts on Geographical Names develop model forms for proposing names of undersea features and Antarctic geographical entities for consideration by national names authorities, patterned after those used by the United States Board on Geographic Names and by similar organizations in other countries, and a form or forms for use by a national names authority in notifying any interested countries or institutions of its intention to name an undersea or Antarctic feature.

II/24   Standardization of names beyond a single sovereignty

The Conference,

Recognizing the increased tempo and volume of research and investigations of the world, the ocean, Antarctica and space, including the moon and the solar planets,

Recognizing further that the absence of an international convention or any other international document determining the rules and procedures of naming and designating features beyond a single sovereignty presents an obstacle to production and application of maps and other documents for international use,

Considering that a special document elaborated under the auspices of the United Nations might provide a general base for adopting technical rules and procedures for the naming and renaming of various kinds of extraterrestrial topographic features and geographical features beyond a single sovereignty,

<u>Recommends</u> that the United Nations Group of Experts on Geographical Names give consideration to the elaboration of such a document in collaboration with the corresponding United Nations bodies and other international organizations competent in this problem.

II/25   Names of features beyond a single sovereignty

<u>The Conference,</u>

<u>Considering</u> the necessity of an international standardization of names of geographical features which are under the sovereignty of more than one country or are divided among two or more countries,

1.   <u>Recommends</u> that countries sharing a given geographical feature under a different name form should endeavour to reach agreement on fixing a single name for the feature concerned;

2.   <u>Further recommends</u> that when countries sharing a given geographical feature and having different official languages do not succeed in agreeing on a common name form, it should be a general rule of international cartography that the name forms of each of the languages in question should be accepted. A policy of accepting only one or some of such name forms while excluding the rest on principle would be inconsistent as well as inexpedient in practice. Only technical reasons may sometimes make it necessary, especially in the case of small-scale maps, to dispense with the use of certain name forms belonging to one language or another.

**II/26   Standardization of names of undersea features beyond a
single sovereignty**

I

The Conference,

Recognizing the importance of the international standardization of
names of undersea features beyond a single sovereignty,

Recognizing further the absence nowadays of a definite system and
procedure for naming such features,

Recommends that the United Nations Group of Experts on Geographical
Names, in co-operation with the appropriate national and international
organizations and, in particular, with the International Hydrographic
Organization, draw up a system for naming undersea features beyond a
single sovereignty and propose it as a basis for preparing an international
convention on the subject.

II

The Conference,

Noting that problems of terminology of undersea features inhibit
international standardization of geographical names employing these
terms,

Noting further the discussions on terminology of undersea features that
are in progress among various countries and with the oceanography
profession,

Recommends that the United Nations Group of Experts on Geographical
Names, in co-operation with interested national names authorities and
international organizations, attempt to standardize the definitions of
undersea feature terms and definitions and to promote their acceptance
and use by names authorities.

II/34 International standardization of names beyond a single sovereignty

The Conference,

Having discussed the problems of the international standardization of geographical names, Having agreed that its field of application extends to the establishment of standardized names of geographical entities lying beyond a single sovereignty,

Recommends that the United Nations Group of Experts on Geographical names continue to study this wider aspect.

III/20 Names of features beyond a single sovereignty

The Conference,

Recommends that resolution 25 of the Second United Nations Conference on the Standardization of Geographical Names be reworded as follows:

The Conference,

"Considering the need for international standardization of names of geographical features that are under the sovereignty of more than one country or are divided among two or more countries,

"1.   Recommends that countries sharing a given geographical feature under different names should endeavour, as far as possible, to reach agreement on fixing a single name for the feature concerned; "

"2.   Further recommends that when countries sharing a given geographical feature do not succeed in agreeing on a common name, it should be a general rule of international cartography that the name used by each of the countries concerned will be accepted. A policy of accepting only one or some of such names while excluding the rest would be inconsistent in principle as well as inexpedient in practice. Only technical reasons may sometimes make it necessary, especially in the case of small-scale maps, to dispense with the use of certain names belonging to one language or another."

V/25   Features beyond a single sovereignty

The Conference,

Recalling resolution 25 of the Second United Nations Conference on the Standardization of Geographical Names,

Considering that it would be useful to know and compare the practical experience acquired by neighbouring countries in the standardization of names of geographical features extending across their common borders,

1.   Recommends that Member States systematically inform future United Nations conferences on the standardization of geographical names of their achievements in this field;

2.   Recommends to that end that those national geographical names authorities that have not yet done so establish with neighbouring authorities joint or interrelated programmes for the collection and treatment of names of features extending across their common borders.

5.   Exonyms

II/28   Lists of exonyms (conventional names, traditional names)

The Conference,

Desiring to facilitate the international standardization of geographical names,

Recognizing that certain exonyms (conventional names, traditional names) form living and vital parts of languages,

Recognizing further that certain exonyms (conventional names, traditional names) remain in the language after the need for them has diminished,

Recommends that national geographical names authorities prepare lists of exonyms currently employed, review them for possible deletions, and publish the results. II/29 Exonyms

I

The Conference,

Recognizing the desirability of limiting the use of exonyms,

Recommends that, within the international standardization of geographical names, the use of those exonyms designating geographical entities falling wholly within one State should be reduced as far and as quickly as possible.

II

The Conference,

Recognizing that exonyms are losing ground, even in national use,

1.   Recommends that in publications intended only for national use the reduction of exonyms should be considered;

2.   Further recommends that in those cases where exonyms are retained, the local official forms should be shown in addition as far as possible.

II/35   Interim lists of standardized names

The Conference,

Recognizing that the final publication of full national gazetteers may not be immediately possible in some countries,

Further recognizing the necessity for having a basic stock of standardized names available for international use,

Considering the keen interest expressed by various countries in abolishing exonyms and using nationally standardized names, and in order to accelerate this process,

1.   Recommends that, in the interim, countries be encouraged to publish concise lists of their names of geographical entities, including administrative divisions, within a reasonable time;

2.   Recommends further that, as far as possible, where these names are officially written in a non-Roman script for which a romanization system has been agreed at the first or Second United Nations Conference on the Standardization of Geographical Names, romanized names in accordance with those systems should be included in the lists.

III/18   Study of exonyms

The Conference,

Noting that, in accordance with resolution 28 of the Second United Nations Conference on the Standardization of Geographical Names, progress has been made in the matter of exonyms in so far as a number of countries have identified and prepared, or are preparing, lists of their own exonyms,

Recognizing, nevertheless, that progress has not been uniform in all countries,

Further recognizing that the reduction of both different types of languages and different linguistic categories of exonyms require different approaches,

Recommends that (a) The countries concerned continue to work on the preparation of provisional lists of exonyms, singling out those suitable for early deletion; (b) The Group of Experts contribute to the exchange of information among the countries concerned on the results of the studies of different categories of exonyms made by those countries.

III/19   Lists of exonyms

The Conference,

Considering that resolution 28 of the Second United Nations Conference on the Standardization of Geographical Names calls for each country to prepare a list of exonyms currently employed,

Noting the definition of the word "exonym" given in the document E/CONF.69/L.1, worked out by that Conference,23

Further noting that the implementation of resolution 28 in its present form must result in enormous lists of doubtful value,

Recommends that the lists referred to in resolution 28 should not contain the following categories of exonyms: those differing from the official name only by the omission, addition or alteration of diacritics or the article; those differing from the official name by declension or derivation; those created by the translation of a generic term.

IV/20   Reduction of exonyms

The Conference,

Noting that, in accordance with resolutions 18 and 19 of the Third United Nations Conference on the Standardization of Geographical Names, further progress has been made in the reduction of the number of exonyms used and a number of States have prepared lists of their own exonyms,

Realizing that the reduction of exonyms used has not been carried out with the same intensity by all States,

Realizing further that the methods and principles aimed at a reduction of the number of exonyms used should constantly be reviewed for expeditious implementation of the resolution and understanding that not all countries can govern the content of maps and atlases published within their territories,

Recommends that exonyms giving rise to international problems should be used very sparingly and published in parenthesis with the nationally accepted standard name.

V/13   Precedence of national official forms of geographical names

The Conference,

Recalling resolution 28 of the Second United Nations Conference on the Standardization of Geographical Names and resolution 20 of the Fourth United Nations Conference on the Standardization of Geographical Names,

Noting that progress has been made in reducing the use of exonyms in cartography and related fields,

Observing that the reduction in the use of exonyms is being carried out at different rates in different countries, Considering that many public and private organizations other than names authorities play a significant and effective role in the dissemination of foreign place names,

1.   Recommends a further reduction in the use of exonyms;

2.   Recommends, more specifically, that countries intensify their efforts to persuade private and public organizations, such as educational institutions, transport companies and the media, to reduce the use of exonyms in their publications or, at least, to increase the use of geographical names in their local standardized form (that is, endonyms);

3.   Also recommends that, where exonyms are used in publications, maps and other documents, precedence be given to national official names.

VIII/4   Working Group on Exonyms of the United Nations Group of Experts on Geographical Names

The Conference,

Recalling resolutions 28, 29, 31 and 38 of the Second United Nations

Conference on the Standardization of Geographical Names, resolutions 18 and 19 of the Third Conference, resolution 20 of the Fourth Conference and resolution 13 of the Fifth Conference, as well as resolutions 4 and 10 of the First Conference, resolution 35 of the Second Conference, resolution 7 of the Third Conference and resolution 4 of the Fourth Conference,

Noting that, notwithstanding the general goal of limiting the use of exonyms, in several countries there has been a tendency to increase their number,

Recognizing that measures such as the categorization of exonym use, the publication of pronunciation guides for endonyms, and the formulation of guidelines ensuring a politically sensitive use of exonyms would help in the reduction of the number of exonyms,

Recommends the establishment of a Working Group on Exonyms of the United Nations Group of Experts on Geographical Names, with the aim of preparing such measures as mentioned above.

Index

INDEX

nominal scale 18
North Sea 42, 74, 186, 187, 188
Northeast Asian History Foundation 4, 5,
  11, 83, 213
Norwegian Sea 53, 54, 55

| O |

ordinal scale 19
Oriental Sea 77, 201, 220

| P |

P.G Chanlaire 207
Pacific Ocean 48, 61, 63, 132, 137, 210
Paldo-Chongdo 195, 197
Pas de Calais 197
PCGN 191
Persian gulf 21, 46, 53
Philippine Sea 53, 54, 55
policy of Primary Local Usage 69
Ptolemy 23, 46, 63

| Q |

quantitative scale 19

| R |

R. Bonne 208
Red Sea 42, 45
Robert de Vaugondy 205, 206
Robert Dudely 206

| S |

Sea of Galilee 21, 44
Sea of Japan 6, 7, 8, 10, 12, 13, 21, 27, 31,
  33, 35, 37, 39, 46, 48, 53, 55, 57, 59, 61, 63,
  64, 65, 66, 67, 68, 70, 71, 72, 73, 76, 77, 78,
  80, 81, 82, 85, 86, 87, 88, 89, 90, 91, 92, 93,
  94, 95, 97, 98, 99, 103, 104, 113, 114, 117,
  131, 132, 134, 135, 136, 154, 157, 160,
  161, 162, 167, 168, 169, 171, 172, 181,
  182, 183, 185, 186, 188, 190, 193, 194,
  196, 199, 201, 202, 203, 205, 209, 210,
  211, 212, 215, 217, 218, 219, 220, 221,
  223, 224, 225, 226
Sea of Korea 46, 75, 76, 90, 95, 133, 134,
  161, 162, 167, 220
Sea of Okhotsk 61, 119, 120, 128, 132,
  133, 134, 135, 136
simultaneous use 168, 226
South China Sea 53, 54, 55, 170
standardization of geographical names
  8, 9, 10, 26, 28, 29, 30, 31, 37, 40, 47, 49,
  50, 65, 67, 93, 95, 96, 97, 99, 100, 141,
  143, 144, 146, 149, 150, 152, 173, 180,
  182, 203, 204, 220, 224, 229, 233, 237,
  238, 239, 240, 241, 242, 243, 244, 245,
  246, 247, 249, 250, 251, 252, 257, 258,
  259, 260, 261, 262, 263, 264

| T |

Taiwan Strait 53, 54, 56
Takahashi Kageyasu 162, 163
Tartar Strait 61
territorial waters 27, 31, 32, 33, 34, 35, 48,
  62, 94, 96, 97, 98, 99, 141, 144, 145, 151,
  195, 196, 197, 198, 199, 203
the English Channel 41, 197
the Society for the East Sea 11, 223, 224,
  225